FRIENDLY FIRE

FRIENDLY FIRE

The remarkable story of a journalist kidnapped in Iraq,
rescued by an Italian secret service agent,
and shot by U.S. forces

GIULIANA SGRENA

Translated by Lesley Freeman Riva
Edited by William Keach

Haymarket
Books

Chicago, Illinois

© 2005, 2006 by Giangiacomo Feltrinelli
First published in 2005 by Giangiacomo Feltrinelli, Italy

This edition published in 2006 by
Haymarket Books
P.O. Box 180165, Chicago, IL 60618
www.haymarketbooks.org

This book was published with the generous support of the Wallace Global Fund.

Distributed to the trade by Consortium Book Sales and Distribution,
www.cbsd.com.

LIBRARY OF CONGRESS CATALOGING-IN-PUBLICATION DATA
Sgrena, Giuliana.
[Fuoco amico. English]
Friendly fire : the remarkable story of a journalist kidnapped in Iraq, rescued by an
Italian secret service agent, and shot by U.S. forces / Giuliana Sgrena ; translated by
Lesley Freeman Riva ; edited by William Keach.
p. cm.
"First published in 2005 by Feltrinelli, Ltd., Italy."
ISBN-13: 978-1-931859-39-4
ISBN-10: 1-931859-39-6
1. Iraq War, 2003---Personal narratives, Italian. 2. Sgrena, Giuliana--Kidnapping,
2005. 3. Iraq War, 2003---Journalists. I. Title.
DS79.76.S47 2006
956.7044'3092--dc22
[B]
2006013912

Printed in Canada

2   4   6   8   10   9   7   5   3   1

CONTENTS

FOREWORD BY AMY GOODMAN AND DENIS MOYNIHAN 7
A NOTE ON THE TRANSLATION 11
INTRODUCTION TO THE NORTH AMERICAN EDITION 13

1. ABDUCTION 17
2. TIME 37
3. LIFE-DEATH 47
4. WAR 65
5. RESISTANCE 83
6. RELIGION 101
7. WOMEN 117
8. ANOTHER LEBANON 133
9. THE ACCIDENT 155
10. ITALY 169
11. CONCLUSIONS 185

APPENDIXES 189
INDEX 209

©University of Alabama

FOREWORD

by AMY GOODMAN
and DENIS MOYNIHAN

GIULIANA SGRENA is a courageous journalist. She has been kidnapped. She has been shot. The story of her abduction and liberation depicts but one in a series of risks she has taken to bring to her readers the stories that too often go untold, of people threatened by war and conflict.

Giuliana Sgrena and journalists like her are committed to these vital stories, to going beyond the official spokespeople and the staged press events. Solo, independent, inviting risk without concern or expectation for reward: this is how all journalists should be. But independent journalists are now increasingly being targeted.

More media workers have been killed or kidnapped in Iraq than in any other conflict in history. The U.S. military began its controversial policy of "embedding" journalists for the 2003 invasion and occupation of Iraq. Of eighty-seven journalists and media workers killed in Iraq by early 2006, only four were U.S. military "embeds"; the rest were independent, unembedded, or as the Pentagon calls them, "unilaterals."

Any journalist heading to Iraq to cover the horror of the occupation there would have to assess the relative risks of working independently versus as an embed. The odds of being killed as a unilateral are currently fifteen times higher than as an embed. So why would anyone go to Iraq to report independently? Embedded journalists assure us that the close quarters with U.S. soldiers, including eating, sleeping, digging foxholes, and agreeing up front to self-censorship, has no influence on their reporting.

Embedded reporter David Bloom of NBC News said this about his embedding experience, in response to questioning from NBC's Lester Holt:

> BLOOM: As a journalist, obviously we're trying to maintain our objectivity and report factually what we see and hear here and not to become one with the force, if you will, because we still have to maintain that appropriate journalistic distance.
>
> As a person, I can tell you that these soldiers have been amazing to us. They have done anything and everything that we could ask of them. And we, in turn, are trying to return the favor by doing anything and everything that they can ask of us. But as far as the relationship is concerned, we are about as one with this force as you could possibly be. We've been going out with these soldiers from the US Army's 3rd Infantry Division since December. We built relationships. We built trust. And I think that now they trust us and we trust them.
>
> Again, as a journalist you have to maintain some distance. If there are problems that they encounter, we'll report those as well and let you know what's going on here, both the good things and the bad things. But just as a human being, they couldn't be anymore generous.... If you accept that they're willing to wrap us in their embrace, if you will, it's a relationship that so far has exceeded my greatest hopes.

(Bloom died in Iraq, reportedly of a blood clot unrelated to combat, although there was some speculation that the clot may have been a complication of the smallpox vaccination he received as a part of his embedding.)

Giuliana Sgrena has made her courageous career one of embedding with the victims of conflict. Prior to her kidnapping, as she eloquently describes, she sought stories from refugees from the U.S. siege of Falluja, one of the least-covered and most devastating U.S. military operations in Iraq. Very few journalists were in Falluja in November of 2004, when the the U.S. military bombed much of Falluja into rubble. But Sgrena was interviewing Fallujans, people who had witnessed the death and destruction, who had buried their loved ones in the soccer stadium, who had fled to Baghdad to live in the mean conditions of a makeshift refugee camp. Here were the eyewitness accounts that would help people in the West grasp the full impact of their governments' actions.

But then Giuliana Sgrena disappeared. Kidnapped. Gone. Yet demonstrating her remarkable discipline as a journalist, even as a prisoner, Sgrena tried to learn about her captors, carefully observing and listening while also trying to avoid provoking them in order to stay alive. She understood well the daily duress under which ordinary Iraqis existed. Whatever was happening to her, was occurring daily in Iraq; one report recently put the number of kidnappings in Iraq at close to thirty per day. But her ordeal was deemed newsworthy by the Western press, since she was Italian. She felt a responsibility to convey not only the details of her ordeal, but the ordeal of so many Iraqis who shared her fate.

After her dramatic release, during which Italian official Nicola Calipari was shot dead by American troops, it would have been easy to flee home and remove herself from the crises in Iraq. But Sgrena has stayed true to her mission to tell the world of the plight of those affected by the violence. "Civilians are the principal victims of modern wars, fought with 'smart bombs' that aren't so smart after all," she writes. "Women and children caught in bombing raids, that's who makes up the majority of victims of the American invasion."

As she recuperated from the gunshot wound she suffered after being fired on by the U.S. military, I interviewed Sgrena on *Democracy Now!*, asking her, "Why did you go to Iraq to begin with? It was a dangerous place. You knew that."

Her answer was simple: "I am a journalist. I went to Somalia. I went to Afghanistan. I went to Algeria. I went everyplace. And I went to Iraq also. I can't go only where the places are not dangerous. It is our work that is dangerous."

When the U.S. invasion and occupation of Iraq began, in March of 2003, we received a comment from a listener of Radio Skid Row, a small community radio station in Sydney, Australia that carries *Democracy Now!* "How is it that the poorest radio station in Sydney is providing the best coverage of the war?" the listener asked.

We believe that it is no coincidence, that independent media and unembedded journalists bring out the stories that resonate with people, that give people the news and information they need to understand these momentous events.

We live in an era when those with the guns are shooting the messenger—and doing it with impunity. Against enormous odds, Giuliana Sgrena is a survivor—a messenger who has been shot but who has lived to tell the tale. She understands in the most personal way the fear, suffering, and courage of the victims and survivors who she covers. Sgrena has risked her life to bring us these stories. Listen to her message.

NOTE ON THE TRANSLATION

FRIENDLY FIRE is a book written in close proximity to the traumatic events at the heart of its story. Every effort has been made to convey in English the style and tone of the Italian text—and especially the voice of Giuliana Sgrena herself. In keeping with this objective, the translation preserves historically specific information as it appears in the original instead of trying to "update" this aspect of the book. In cases where knowledge of subsequent developments or additional data might be helpful, especially to non-Italian readers, brief supplements to the original are included in the text within square brackets. Giuliana Sgrena read the final draft of the translation in its entirety; her corrections and clarifications were incorporated into the version printed here.

One of the challenges in translating *Friendly Fire* had to do with differences between Italian and English political terminology. An especially significant example is the Italian word *pacifista*, which is used several times by Sgrena to characterize her own political stance. In these instances "pacifist" is the appropriate English equivalent, even though American "pacifism," with its considerable influence from Quaker and other protestant religious doctrines of nonviolence, is not identical with either the secular or the Roman Catholic traditions within Italian "pacifism." But Sgrena also uses *pacifista* to designate the broader movement opposed to the U.S. war on and occupation of Iraq—as in *movimento pacifista*. In these cases, "peace movement" or "antiwar movement" is a more accurate translation, since the movement includes both those opposed in principle to all forms of political violence and those who are not. Other less prominent differences between Italian and English political terminology are dealt with through brief, bracketed clarifications within the text.

INTRODUCTION TO THE
NORTH AMERICAN EDITION

OVER THE past months, as I've participated in various initiatives against the war, I've had the occasion to meet members of the U.S. military who had fought in Iraq and are now denouncing the disastrous effects of that conflict, just as I've met family members of soldiers who were killed in that country or who passed months in jail as conscientious objectors. There was an instant solidarity between us, naturally. They told of how they were forced to carry out orders—and I'm sure that whoever shot at us the night of March 4, 2005, in Baghdad was also just carrying out orders, or following senseless rules of engagement. In the end, he too (or they, if there was more than one) is a victim of this war. This is why, although I'd do anything to know the truth of what happened that night, I have no thirst for vengeance, I have no desire to find a scapegoat. On the contrary: I'd like to meet the soldier who shot at us and killed Nicola Calipari in order to know what he was thinking at that moment, what induced him to open fire, what he felt in the aftermath. Maybe this encounter is impossible. It may never happen, but I harbor the illusion that it might serve us both.

I have a goal in common with these ex-U.S. soldiers and the parents of the victims: putting an end to the war, and denouncing all its perverse effects. Condemnation of the war by those who participated directly in the occupation has a powerful impact on the U.S. public, even on that segment of the public that believed their own country to be in danger and accepted the war as a way of confronting that danger. The facts demonstrate the contrary, however, and the victims continue to pile up, on both sides. This kind of conscious-ness-raising is extremely important, since the U.S. military is the principal occupier of Iraq, and George W. Bush the principal sup-porter of the war launched in 2003 against Saddam, under the false pretext of weapons of mass destruction that Iraq no longer pos-sessed. Instead, it was the invading military forces that brought chemical weapons (napalm, phosphorus) and used them against the civilian Iraqi population. All are accomplices and responsible for the massacres, the torture, and the violation of international conven-tions and the rights of the Iraqi people.

In light of recent events, unfortunately, it is now clear that in the space of a few months the most pessimistic predictions contained in the Italian draft of this book, which foresaw a slide into civil war, have been confirmed—the civil war that occupying forces feared would be the result if they were to withdraw. The occupying troops are still in Iraq, but the civil war is already taking a heavy toll of vic-tims. And every day, the number of Iraqi victims, never accounted for, far exceeds that of foreigners.

How to put an end to this daily bloodshed? I think the only way to break the cycle of violence is the withdrawal of all troops. On this point, peace movements all over the world are united. A withdrawal would not immediately restore peace—at first, it might even inten-sify the clashes between the various Iraqi factions—but it would cer-tainly strip away the alibi of those using violence to fight the occupiers, and above all, of the terrorists, who are not interested in the liberation of Iraq, but are using the Iraqi territory to fight their

Jihad (holy war), not so much against foreigners but against the Shiite "traitors" (as they are considered by Sunni fundamentalists).

Yet, Iraq cannot be abandoned in its current war-ravaged condition. Once they regain their sovereignty, the Iraqis must be helped to rebuild their country, a task that cannot be done with tanks and Apache helicopters. Holding out the prospect of jobs and development to the Iraqis could be another way of defusing the violence.

These are some of the points contained in this book. It is not limited to describing my dramatic experience, first as a hostage, and then as a victim of American fire. Both, for me, were cases of "friendly fire," as the title says—friendly fire from the U.S. soldiers against Italian allies, and the "fire" of my abductors against a journalist engaged in the movement against the war and the occupation. Instead, the book is dedicated above all to Iraq, to the living conditions I shared with the Iraqis, to the economic, political, and military situation. And to the Islamization under way, to the increasing territorial control by fanatical religious militias who are changing the secular face of Iraq, and imposing Shari'a before it has ever been declared law. The principal victims of this situation are women, to whom I devoted an entire chapter.

My goal is to contribute to the understanding of a country that remains largely unknown to international public opinion—not least because it is no longer possible to report on Iraq, and in particular, to report independently. None of the sides participating in the armed conflict want witnesses, so all of Iraqi civil society is forced into isolation. An entire population held hostage by belligerents. For anyone who has been a hostage, it is doubly frustrating.

Giuliana Sgrena
Rome, April 13, 2006

ONE

ABDUCTION

"WHO CAN guarantee that you're not a spy?" A man stares at me with light, glacial eyes under a white-and-red-checked kaffiyeh. I take the bait: "Nobody can guarantee that I'm not a spy, least of all me: I'm a journalist. I've come here to gather stories from the refugees of Falluja. If you trust me, talk—otherwise, hold your tongue." Ahmad doesn't back down. He repeats a few well-known facts, like the occupation of the General Hospital at the beginning of the American attack against Falluja, which, he adds, came "when a woman was giving birth: she was abandoned there with the umbilical cord still to be cut!" I ask if he was in Falluja during the attack, but he says he was in a Baghdad hospital during that period for a problem with his leg, and his family was with him to help. It's useless to explain that I want him to give me fresh details, stories that haven't already been covered. He just keeps repeating anti-American slogans, while he stares into my eyes threateningly. Later, I'll find out that he had asked my driver if I had an escort—an armed escort, he meant.

The climate was hostile, tremendously hostile, but I couldn't let that dissuade me from telling the story of the destruction of Falluja through the memories and images of the people who had lived through it, or through the stories of their relatives trapped by the siege. Up to that moment the news—what there was of it—was reaching us exclusively through journalists embedded with American troops. The censorship had not, however, been able to prevent the scoop of NBC reporter Kevin Sites, who had filmed a marine killing a wounded and unarmed combatant as he lay on the floor of a Falluja mosque. Although the images he captured had flashed around the world, Kevin Sites had been expelled from the group of embedded journalists because he had not respected the "rules of engagement" and of censorship. Some time later the marine involved in the shooting would be absolved for having acted "in legitimate defense." Other journalists recruited for the Falluja assignment assured me they would never want to repeat the experience. They were spared nothing: not even the work of digging trenches.

Falluja had been an obsession of mine for years, not just during this last trip to Baghdad. I had "discovered" the story at the end of April 2003, after the first revolt that had made the city a symbol of resistance against the occupation. I returned there on every subsequent trip to Iraq. I had met willing sources with whom a real friendship and collaboration was born. They were convinced of the necessity of telling the world about the reality of Falluja, and so they helped me with my work. Usually, a meeting would take place at the house of Abu Mohammed, but each time I came others would be convened (telephones were still working in Falluja at that time). We'd all sit on the floor in the large living room, following tribal tradition, and discuss the latest events. Mustafa, a mechanic, was always the best informed: since my first visit, he'd been telling me of how, right after the battle for the airport, one of the bloodiest of the occupation of Baghdad, he had gone to search for the bodies of his relatives and found the corpses carbonized, burned beyond recognition. The question arose right away: what weapons had been used? Napalm? Phosphorus?

Yet since the previous June (of 2004, before the so-called transfer of power to the "provisional Iraqi government"), Falluja had been off-limits, an isolation imposed after the first heavy American attacks in April had infuriated the population. The various resistance groups had divided themselves along political, tribal, and religious lines, radicalizing their positions. The isolation imposed by the occupiers had favored the arrival of foreign Arabs. "We know there are foreign fighters," a boy told me after escaping from Falluja in September of 2004, when the city was already being targeted for bombing, "but we never had any contact with them."

From then on I had rarely been able to contact my friends by phone. Finally, in the attack of November 2004, their house had been reduced to rubble. What had happened to them? Had they too ended up in the endless lines of refugees? Probably, but where? I had no further news.

Thus even before the national elections—the event that had brought me to Iraq at the end of January 2005—I had been searching for refugees from Falluja, those who had escaped before or during the attack. And since I was unable to find my former contacts, I had to explore other avenues. It wasn't easy. Mohammed, a friend who works with an Italian NGO that delivers aid to the evacuees of that tortured city, had put me on guard: "I won't take you to the Fallujan refugees. It's too dangerous. They're very angry, they don't want to see anyone, and they barely trust other Iraqis, never mind Westerners!" I have always had a lot of respect for Mohammed's opinion—he has helped me in many difficult moments—but I thought he was exaggerating about the refugees, perhaps as a form of hyperprotectiveness.

The terror of abduction had changed the lives of Iraqis as well: already, when I was in Baghdad back in September during the saga of [the two kidnapped Italian aid workers] Simona Torretta and Simona Pari, Mohammed did not even want to know my plans or itinerary. "If they seized my children, I don't know what my reaction would be," he repeated, and so he preferred to remain in the dark about my movements. He would call me often throughout the day, however, to see if I was "still in one piece," as he put it.

Obviously, I wasn't the only one interested in Falluja, and a friend of mine, a photographer, gave me a tip on where to find a camp of Fallujan refugees. The place was the Mustafa Mosque, located on the campus of Nahrein University. This was the ex-Saddam University that had been rebaptized the "University of the Two Rivers" (the Tigris and the Euphrates) after the fall of the regime. The mosque, which looks from a distance like an enormous green shell, is at the edge of the large campus, isolated from the academic buildings. Around the dome, tents had been set up to shelter Fallujan refugees, maybe fifteen hundred in all. Other tents, transformed into a sort of yellow canvas screen, had crept right inside the edifice to protect the poor evacuees from the cold and rain: women on one side, men on the other.

Upon my arrival, with my interpreter and driver (both of them Sunni—in occupied Iraq, the choice of escorts is a detail that can't be taken lightly), the men are gathered, talking in small groups, while the women move about with pots and basins followed by flocks of children spattered with mud. It is Friday—February 4, 2005—and it is raining. The image of the camp is even more wretched and miserable than usual. But as the morning draws to a close, a few beams of sunlight allow the faithful to drag green prayer rugs outside the mosque to escape the cold and damp of the interior. There is a little time before prayers, however. Thanks to the authorization of the imam, Sheikh Hussein, who had let us know that he was busy with the preparation of his sermon, I try to break through the curtain of hostility that surrounds me. I am heedless of Ahmad's group, none of whom let me out of their sight. I don't want to give up. I know the suffering of these people—I had been in Falluja the day after a bombing raid—and I am sure I can get past their distrust. Besides, I have visited refugee camps all over, from Somalia to Kurdistan, in conditions even worse than these. In all of them I'd seen the anger of powerlessness or resignation, but I'd always been well received—never had I run up against such distrust and hostility (and the line between the two emotions, after all, is extremely thin) as among the evacuees of Falluja. I remember a moment right after the first Gulf War, when I arrived at a refugee camp of Iraqi Kurds in Turkey where cholera was rampant. They had greeted me with a mug of water, which I could not refuse despite the risk of contagion—it was the only thing they had to offer. The gesture was a sign of hospitality.

The situation now is different: even though we find ourselves in the courtyard of a mosque, there's no room for traditional hospitality. I realize that all Westerners are perceived as enemies because they are associated, without exception, with the occupiers, and are thus responsible for the destruction of Falluja. As Italians, it has been difficult for some time to separate ourselves from the choices of our government: at the beginning of the war the climate and sensibilities were different, but today, after two years of occupation, souls have inevitably become embittered. The mediation of Sheikh Hussein, who is himself from Falluja, has served only to allow me to enter the camp, not to protect me. But for the moment, I'm not worried.

I'm not worried, because some of these refugees want, indeed need, to talk, to tell their stories. Abdallah, a twenty-six-year-old, begins. He had returned to Falluja with his brother, just before the attack. Both of them had been selling gasoline on the black market, one of the most lucrative activities during the occupation. They had to clear out their house, where they had stockpiled jerricans of fuel, otherwise the first bomb would have turned their home into a raging bonfire. Once they had moved the gas to safety, a friend had indicated the only way, the single road that remained open to escape from Falluja. Their friend, Majid, remained behind: he couldn't leave his people, he said. An ambulance driver, he joined his colleagues— twenty-three in all—in a makeshift emergency room. The bombing had been going on for some time—this was November 8, 2004—and Majid had gathered with his colleagues to organize rescue efforts for the wounded when a bomb hit the building where the rescuers were sheltered: only seven of the twenty-three present were saved.

The situation went from bad to worse. After a few days, corpses began to fill the streets. Not only was there no electricity or water, but food became increasingly scarce. To fill their bellies, dogs began to gnaw the cadavers lying in the streets. And the human beings? Those still cowering behind the walls of their houses, too frightened to look out the window, terrorized by the bombs and nauseated by the stench of the corpses?

One day—recounted Majid—the American troops took a megaphone and invited the whole neighborhood (those left alive, shut up in their houses) to head toward a gathering spot where they were told they'd find Red Crescent (the Islamic Red Cross) volunteers distributing aid. Cut off from the world, they had no way of knowing that the Red Crescent had actually been prevented from entering the city to offer help. So off they marched, in two separate lines—men on one side and women and children on another—toward a mirage, passing by the dog-gnawed corpses abandoned in the streets.

Instead of help, however, the men found handcuffs. They were all considered combatants; hence, they were roughly interrogated and locked up in a camp. It took several days for Majid, along with a few others, to be released, and he was only freed after proving that he had not touched explosives (with a paraffin glove test). But free to go where? Wandering alone and desperate, he headed toward the mosque, usually a place of refuge. Not in this case: the floor was covered with bodies. The Americans had killed all the young men seeking shelter in the place of prayer, an old caretaker told him—he himself had been spared only because of his advanced age. Desperate and nauseated, Majid had no idea where to go. It was the old caretaker who pointed him to a nearby house where an old man and three women were still living with a bunch of children. After feeding him, however, the man asked him to leave: "If the Americans find you, they'll kill us all," the man told him. So Majid was on the run again, without a destination, searching for an escape route. Eventually he was able to cross the river, dodging the American bullets intended for fugitives, until he reached his own family in Baghdad. Abdallah doesn't want to say any more, but he gives the impression of telling in third person a story that is really his, a story he knows only too well. Probably it's a precaution—he too feels the watchful eyes of the group of men who have been keeping us constantly within range.

In the meantime, some children sidle up to us followed by their mothers. The little girls, so small, are already veiled, and the young women are covered from head to toe by black veils with just two eye holes. "Did you cover yourselves this way in Falluja?" I ask. "No, before, no, but we know it pleases Sheikh Hussein," they respond.

Falluja, called the "city of mosques," boasts madrassas (Koranic schools) that offer the most prestigious Sunni religious training in Iraq, like that of Najaf for the Shiites. This religious tradition has transformed Falluja into a highly conservative city: here, not a drop of alcohol has ever been for sale, no cinema or Internet café has ever opened, and the veil is imposed on women by fatwa (Koranic edict). The veil was always a traditional head covering, however, and not a Wahhabi-style garment like that worn by these women in the Mustafa Mosque. In any event, the veil is not posing an obstacle to our conversation—anything but. Without shyness or false modesty, these women pelt me with a barrage of words: they express anger, desperation, powerlessness, but also, above all, dignity. They tell me of all they have lost leaving Falluja behind under the bombs. One of them tells me of trying to rescue her daughter's trousseau, intended for a wedding that had been prevented by the American attack. "One morning," she recounts, "I got in the car with my two children to return home. Eight hours of traveling (the distance between Baghdad and Falluja is about thirty-one miles) … traffic jams, checkpoints, controls…." Residents of Falluja must register not only their fingerprints but also a retinal scan. "When we finally arrived, I found my house destroyed, without doors or windows, and my daughter's dowry cut into shreds … beyond the loss, the defacement. What could I do? I came back here to live in a tent." And the dollars the Americans gave you to rebuild your houses? "What can we do with two hundred dollars for a house that has been destroyed?" Another woman, named Fawzia, went so far as to refuse the money: "I don't want their dirty money, which is our money anyway, since they make it with our oil," she asserts with pride.

Now even that money has run out, eight million dollars distributed among residents. The refugees camped out around the mosque live on handouts, mostly from Iraqis, claims Sheikh Hussein. "The government has given us nothing; on the contrary, they sent in the National Guard." But just as he's saying this a van from an Islamic nongovernmental organization in Qatar pulls up. It unloads cooking oil, tomatoes, sugar, and a few other provisions that the refugees divide up, showing their Saddam-era ration cards from the time of the embargos, now signed by the imam.

At the hour of prayer, 12:30 p.m., a weak sun warms the faithful who spread out on the green carpet: the men in front, women and children behind. But there are some who continue to wander around the camp, sullen and indifferent to the sermon. Like all imams these days, Sheikh Hussein does not shy away from politics— he accuses the Americans of destroying Falluja under the pretext of a hunt for Al Qaeda terrorists. "But where is [Jordanian Al Qaeda leader Abu Mussab al] Zarqawi?" is the rhetorical question he poses to the faithful.

Calmed by the presence of my photographer friend who had showed me the camp, and who had appeared suddenly with the imam before the beginning of prayers (although he left shortly after), I wait till the end of the sermon to thank Sheikh Hussein. I realize I've been at the mosque for quite a while, but leaving the camp without thanking the imam would be an unpardonable discourtesy. Still, it's no easy thing to accomplish. Other men follow the sheikh into a bare building flanking the mosque. It apparently serves as an antechamber to his quarters, from which issue the cries of babies, building in volume when someone opens the door to offer us a Pepsi. And now his cell phone starts ringing: the sheikh pulls from his pocket a phone decorated from top to bottom with religious symbols. Koranic verses have been substituted for the standard ring tone. The contrast between technology and religious orthodoxy is striking, and yet they seem to coexist peacefully. Then, the religious leader hands me a booklet in Arabic about the attack on Falluja, as well as a flyer from a Web site that bears an image of the Al Kabir Mosque in Falluja (bombed during the fighting) with the title "How do we stop the evil of hatred?" Sheikh Hussein appears nervous, at times distracted. Before addressing me, he asks my translator what it's like to work with a female Western journalist. The cleric alternates between Arabic and English, and the others, who have been gradually crowding the room, jump in. In Iraq it's customary for anyone who enters the room to insert himself into or interrupt the discussion underway. I've grown used to it, and I take advantage to elicit opinions from the new arrivals. The climate among the sheikh's followers again grows extremely tense and hostile as we talk about Falluja. An old man with a highly dignified air challenges me: "What can you do for us? Why should we answer you—what does it serve us?" Needless to say, my discourse on the importance of informing international public opinion about the conditions of refugees and the destruction of Falluja, and circulating a different version of events than that controlled by journalists embedded with American troops, is met with extreme skepticism. Falluja has been destroyed; it must be rebuilt. And that requires money, lots of money. It's Sheikh Hussein who quantifies: "We demand the same compensation asked of Gadhafi for the victims of Lockerbie, ten million dollars for every victim of Falluja." "And how many victims are there?" I ask, given that figures now circulating on the number of dead differ wildly, while the wounded are not even counted. Sheikh Hussein throws out a number: five thousand. And then he adds, "combatants." He doesn't dwell on civilians.

"The victims are hard to tally. Nobody could move around the city during those days," remembers Fadhil Badrani, a local journalist who works with Reuters and who remained in Falluja during the bombing. But "a rough estimate made by hospitals, the imams, and residents puts it at more than three thousand...." The bodies were buried "in the gardens of houses, or they just remained under the rubble" (*El Diario*, May 27, 2005). Mohammed Hadeed, one of the first doctors to enter Falluja after the bombing, refers to the assessment of the medical outfit he was with, and calculates that the victims numbered between three thousand and five thousand people. That figure is closer to Sheikh Hussein's numbers than to those of the U.S. military command (who said between twelve thousand and sixteen thousand combatants were killed). In any event, it seems that only seven hundred were identified and buried, while the others ended up in mass graves, gnawed by dogs, or carbonized by American arms.

Evidently, Sheikh Hussein is aiming high: $10 million multiplied by five thousand makes a nice sum. A provocation? No, the sheikh seems convinced of what he says and doesn't backtrack easily. His cell phone rings again, but the imam doesn't even bother to take it out of his pocket. He says he is tired, since he rose at dawn, and he takes his leave quickly. "What is your name?" I ask before leaving. "Just put Hussein, otherwise the National Guard will return." They are words that come back to me often in the next weeks, along with the fact that he did not want to be photographed.

We leave, "escorted" to the gate. I have to call the newspaper. The stories the refugees have told me are certainly no scoop, but they give a hands-on sense of reality—this is my daily mission. Before this, I had met with other Fallujan refugees sheltering with relatives who had already told me of their attempts to return to their city. I met Mohammed in Sadr City—he was not from Falluja, but had moved there under Saddam to work in a truck factory owned by the Ministry of Defense. Mohammed told me that two neighbors of his had returned to Falluja, but were informed by the Americans that their house must first be disinfested. The Americans gave them two drums of a special detergent to do the job. "They told me that they found the apartment covered in a white powder, and when they started to clean it up one of them felt sick—she was bleeding all over." I would have liked to meet those women, but events got in the way.

As we drive away from the Mustafa Mosque, I'm feeling pleased with the morning's work. First I call the newspaper, and as I wait for them to get back to me I decide to call my Italian colleagues here. We have a lunch appointment, and I'll let them know I'm on my way. The appointment is at 2 p.m. I look at my watch: that's in ten minutes. The phone is still ringing when gunshots bring me back to reality. We are outside the mosque gates, and have just passed the security guardhouse of the university without seeing any guards— they have evidently stayed inside because it's Friday and there's not much to do, or perhaps they've been informed of what's about to happen. Suddenly two, maybe three cars pull in front of the cement security barriers and block our exit. My driver, Mohammed, panics and takes off on foot, trying to dodge the bullets of one of the kidnappers. Wael, the translator, is sitting in the front seat, trying uselessly to block the doors of the car. A robust young man rips open the door and drags me away, grabbing my cell phone that has fallen to the floor before the colleague I had been calling has answered. Before my abductor switches it off, my colleague can hear the initial phase of my kidnapping. The man loads me into another car, where there are four people besides me—they jam me in between the two men in the rear seat.

In the face of my protests, the man sitting beside the driver turns, stares straight into my eyes, and says, "Have no fear, we are Muslims." But his gaze, full of hate, does not reassure me. On the contrary. I think back to the eve of the war—the declared war, of aerial bombardments—in March of 2003, when, in a diary for the German weekly Die Zeit, I wrote: "Maybe if they hated us, if they were aggressive toward us, it would be easier to face them. Instead, no. They are gentle but not servile; proud but not arrogant. It is we who are barbarous compared to their civilization, born in Mesopotamia six thousand years ago, which has left its indelible traces on the history of humanity. Those who unleash the bombs will not look into their eyes."

Two years of war and occupation have passed, and here is the result: now I see hate in their eyes. They are no longer gentle. They are still proud, but also violent, and they are abducting me.

I knew the power of war to corrupt had no limits, leading even to the exploitation of civilians and the use of abductions, but now I'm a victim: I feel hostage to my own convictions.

But why me, specifically? I asked myself this every day of my four-week imprisonment. Why seize a journalist who had always fought against the war? Why had interviewing the refugees of Falluja, the most tormented city in Iraq, become a trap? I did not then know that my French colleague Florence Aubenas, a reporter for *Libération*, and her collaborator Hussein had been abducted in exactly the same place just one month before, after interviewing the same refugees. (The two were freed in June 2005.) After my liberation, Sheikh Hussein, who is no longer at the Mustafa Mosque, would get a message to me saying that those who seized me did not belong to the resistance; on the contrary, their actions were ruining the image of the resistance, and the women whom I had met at the camp were very sorry about what had happened to me. My kidnappers denied this, but perhaps it was only after abducting me that they found out who I was and what I had done up until then.

I had arrived in Baghdad in February of 2003 to participate in a global demonstration against the war, held simultaneously all around the world. I stayed on through the bombing, even when all the Western embassies, with the U.S. in the lead, were pressing us to leave and terrorizing us with images of the catastrophic effects of the possible use of weapons of mass destruction. At our insistence, the Italian Embassy had procured kits with masks, protective suits, filters, etc., to face such an eventuality; yet we were forced to leave the bags containing this equipment in the embassy itself. After explanations of the use of the mask and filters had convinced me of their total uselessness, I admit to some feelings of unease. Yet although the sport of the day was indulging in crazy *Star Wars* fantasies that fed the general panic, the idea of abandoning the field never occurred to me. When my newspaper, in an excess of prudence in my regard, asked me to return to Italy, I suddenly felt lost. I was aware of the dangers, but I was not afraid and I wanted to be a witness to what was about to unfold. For me, it was more difficult to leave than to stay. So I stayed. My mission was to report on the daily life of Iraqis, first under the bombs, and then during the occupation—which is nothing less than the continuation of the war.

FALLUJA

Picture a city of more than 250,000 residents at the gates of Baghdad, on the road to Jordan. This position allowed the Fallujans to develop thriving construction and commercial transportation industries. Thanks to these flourishing activities, the city was expanding, with neighborhoods full of new homes and wide, dusty boulevards. This city was almost razed to the ground in the attack of November 2004. According to official Iraqi government sources, 36,955 houses were hit, 3,600 demolished, 2,000 burned, 21,000 occupied. As for the stores and businesses: 1,800 were completely destroyed, 8,400 were damaged, 250 factories were burned. In addition to these damages, according to Doctor Hafid al Dulaimi, head of the Commission for Compensation of Falluja Citizens, 60 daycare centers and schools were hit and 65 mosques and religious sites were damaged. As if this were not enough, the bombing created environmental problems: among other effects, the city's drinking water was contaminated by sewage. Damages calculated by another member of the commission amount to $600 million, but then premier Iyad Allawi recognized only 20 percent, and as of June of last year, had only allocated funds to cover 10 percent. According to Mohammed Hadeed, a Falluja doctor, at least 31,000 city residents are still waiting to be compensated. Many of them had their homes destroyed, and without other shelter have been camping in the ruins.

The November attack against Falluja was part of the "final offensive," which, according to the U.S., was supposed to clear the way for the elections of January 30, 2005. But Operation "al Fajr" (Dawn) excluded not only the residents of Falluja but all Sunnis from the elections. Today, the city is still locked down. Only residents can enter, through six tightly controlled checkpoints and after displaying identification, resulting in hours-long waits. Only 80 percent of the more than 250,000 residents have returned (another reason why it is difficult to calculate the dead and missing).

The American final offensive was preceded by other heavy attacks, above all in the month of April. Instead of reinforcing American control over the city, it led only to Falluja's isolation. The U.S. military wanted to destroy what had become, since April of 2003, a symbol of Iraqi resistance.

As troops were advancing on Falluja after the occupation of Baghdad, the tribal and religious leaders of the city, concerned about the effect foreign soldiers would have on Falluja, put together a delegation to meet with the U.S. military command on April 9, 2003. In the end, they reached an agreement: there would be no opposition to the occupation, but the soldiers would not enter the residential areas, avoiding a major disruption of life in the "city of mosques." But the agreement was not respected: on April 23, marines occupied the al Qaid elementary school, and on April 28, when the population demonstrated against the decision to prevent students from attending school, U.S. soldiers shot at the demonstrators, killing fourteen and critically wounding three. Two days later, there was another demonstration, with another three dead and sixteen wounded. And that's how the Iraqi resistance to the occupation began. In the meantime, the marines set up a base—Camp Baharia—on the outskirts of the city, and patrols and searches soon followed. They mostly moved at night: the marines would storm into houses and drag men, women, and children out of bed at gunpoint. Then the residents would be forced into the street while the marines searched their homes. According to complaints filed by many residents, money and jewelry disappeared during these raids. These accusations were sometimes verified by the soldiers themselves, who maintained that the money was intended to finance the resistance. And if the soldiers did not find what they were looking for—suspected supporters of the ex-dictator and combatants— they would arrest a family member, a son, or occasionally a woman (a practice that continues).

The occupation threw into turmoil a life shaped by tribal-religious conservatism. The Americans were accused, for example, of looking at women with binoculars, or even infrared rays. All of this served to feed the hostility toward the occupiers, which was immediately transformed into armed conflict.

From the beginning of the conflict, Falluja was thus a symbol of resistance to the Iraqis, and an obsession for the Americans.

Downed helicopters, military transports destroyed—the signs are visible all along the highway, where the guardrails are reduced to tangles of twisted metal. Or at least they were visible when it was still possible to travel on the highway from Baghdad to Amman—a trip that has now become too dangerous. The revolt of Falluja also includes appalling episodes like the execution on March 31, 2004, of four contractors working for Blackwater, a security agency hired to protect U.S. ambassador John Negroponte (and also to do any dirty work in which the military doesn't want to be directly involved). The four were killed, mutilated, and dragged around the city before being hung from a bridge that crosses the Euphrates. The American reprisal was ferocious: the city was surrounded by tanks and on April 4 the attack began. Fighting lasted for two weeks and caused at least a thousand deaths, but the Americans did not manage to impose control over Falluja. Despite the use of vast force, the American military suffered a grave setback: on May 10, the city was abandoned into the hands of the Falluja Brigade, under the command of an ex-general of Saddam, Jassim Mohammed Saleh. A native of Falluja, he had a great deal of influence over the population but was not easily manipulated by the Americans. So after a few days they replaced him with an ex-companion-in-arms, General Mohammed Latif, who was less powerful and more compromised by collaboration. Forced to leave Falluja, the Americans wanted at least to rehabilitate the "Saddamist" resistance—an attempt at correcting the gravest error committed by proconsul Paul Bremer, who had dissolved the Iraqi military and the Baath Party upon his arrival in Baghdad—and thus isolate the Islamic faction, with whom General Saleh had allied himself. From the inception of Bremer's rule, the city of mosques has been controlled by various emirs—military, tribal, and religious heads—joined in the *shura*, the counsel of the mujahideen. The council imposes the harshest law: that of shari'a, Koranic law, enforced by Islamic courts that punish "spies" with decapitation. Of the two spiritual leaders of the mujahideen, the more moderate and authoritative is Dhafer al Obeidi of the Handra al Mohammadiya Mosque, and the more radical is Abdullah al Janabi (part of a large and powerful tribe to which Sheikh Hussein of the Mustafa Mosque in Baghdad also belongs). It is the latter who prevails. His fevered sermons delivered from the Saad bin Abi Waqas Mosque are followed by mujahideen from other Arab countries as well. But Sheikh al Janabi refuses any responsibility for the killing of six Shiite truck drivers from Sadr City. The drivers were killed and mutilated on June 5, 2004, as they drove through Falluja, because they were considered collaborators—an episode that greatly undermined the previous solidarity demonstrated by Shiites for the Sunni residents of Falluja during the April 2004 attack.

This is the "liberated territory" that the Wahhabists (fundamentalists of the Saudi school who migrated to Iraq during the last years of the Saddam regime) want to transform into the first emirate of Iraq. The model is Afghanistan under the Taliban, where hooded men hunted down anyone drinking or using drugs, then whipped them in public. If the Americans wanted to isolate the radical Islamic groups, they obtained precisely the opposite effect; so they had to take their revenge under the pretext of hunting down al Zarqawi's terrorists. But the following attack of November 2004, considered by the American press to be "the most ferocious urban battle fought by American soldiers since Vietnam" (*New York Times*, July 15, 2005), with the loss of dozens of soldiers, probably still did not achieve the hoped-for effect. Today, the city is completely locked down, under curfew from 10 p.m. each night. As of July 2005 it is still occupied by 4,300 marines who live in Iraqi houses, patrol streets bordered by rolls of barbed wire and control the six checkpoints that give access to the city. This doesn't stop the guerrillas from attacking the marines daily, inflicting notable losses. The American troops had combed the city house by house during the attack, seizing huge quantities of explosives, but bombs continue to abound. The attacks don't spare Iraqi "collaborators." Members of the new city council and General Mehdi Sabeen Hashin, commander of the 800 paramilitary troops who, together with 2,800 soldiers, constitute the Iraqi military presence in Falluja, have escaped several attacks only by a miracle. Although city residents play down the role of Iraqis in the November attack, their presence is barely tolerated by the Fallujans, who accuse these "Shiites from the south" of maltreatment. Even those who most wish for peace, for a city free of armed factions and Islamic militants, are radicalized: "after the injustice with which the inhabitants of Falluja were treated by the American and Iraqi troops, now they prefer the resistance. At least that way they won't be humiliated," declared Abdul Jabbar Kadhim al Alwani, the owner of a mechanic's shop, to the *New York Times* (July 15, 2005). For American troops, Falluja continues to be a nightmare—and certainly not the only one.

TWO

TIME

It is cold, colder than usual. Winter is harsh in Baghdad, but this day is also damp. It had rained, a rarity in Iraq. The scarf wrapped around my head, which I had put on to enter the mosque, doesn't bother me as it usually does; on the contrary, it warms me and isolates me from what's happening. On Friday the streets are semi-deserted, traffic flows quickly without the daily traffic jams, while I, crushed between my abductors, am taken to my prison. My desperate gaze meets the indifference of the few distracted passersby. It doesn't take long to arrive at the small house, one among many, that is to become my cell. When we arrive "home," my abductors—two have remained—turn on the television, resigning themselves to watching an Iraqi channel after numerous useless attempts to make the satellite work. After little more than a half hour, the anchor on Iraqya TV announces my abduction—with exceptional timeliness, thanks to the Italian news agency ANSA, which had the news in real time (due to my aborted cell phone call). And thus begins a kind of countdown that will end only with my liberation.

From that moment on the notion of time becomes an obsession for me: its perception is compressed or expanded beyond all proportion depending on the occasion. Being deprived of all my personal effects, including my watch, and never knowing the time, increases my disorientation. Sometimes I ask one of my abductors, the one posing as a "bodyguard," what time it is. "Why do you want to know?" he always responds. At the beginning, Hussein—this is what he says to call him—had worn a watch; then evidently he too conformed to the rules of the prison, and to avoid temptation, took it off. The room where I am held for twenty-eight days has no light: a large window is blocked off by some furniture, to prevent any contact, even visual, with the exterior. Therefore I can't even tell if it's day or night. Only in the bathroom, through a small, high window, can I glimpse the alternation of the sun and moon, of day and night. I pass my days in the dark.

It feels like time doesn't pass at all. The hours, the days, the nights are interminable. I can't even sleep. How long will I be held here? How can I hold on to a perception of time? How to count the days? My black pashmina shawl comes to the rescue: I've barely taken it off since I bought it in Pakistan, where I found myself on the eve of the war in Afghanistan, trying to prepare for the rigors of the Afghan cold. As I write this, I no longer have that shawl: when I returned home, it was missing from the effects handed over in a black plastic bag by the American military hospital at Camp Victory. The shawl has a long fringe, and for every day I pass in captivity, I knot one of the threads. The first day I made four knots, so I'd remember it was the fourth of February, the day of my abduction—as if it were possible to forget! I count the number of possible knots—seventy-three on one side and seventy-three on the other—sincerely hoping that my imprisonment will finish first. Each day I wait for what I assume is afternoon before making a new knot, since I was abducted around 2 p.m. Paradoxically, in these conditions such meticulousness becomes a point of honor.

But how to calculate the interminable dragging of the hours? The only help I have is the muezzin of a mosque who calls the faithful to prayer five times a day: at five thirty in the morning, at twelve thirty in the afternoon, at three, five thirty, and seven thirty at night. Sometimes the calls are quite distinct, other times they get lost in the wind, a sign that the mosque must not be so close after all. These are the only signs that give any rhythm to the flow of time and interrupt the aimless wandering of my mind. My abductors respect these calls as well, since I hear them praying in the next room, particularly in the morning, when noises from the street don't yet grant any distraction.

Even meals don't have their usual regularity; evidently they depend on other circumstances. And after my continual refusals of food—in the first three days I managed to swallow just some orange juice, tea, and a biscuit or two—my abductors leave it to me to tell them when I want to eat. So I let it go. When I eat, the menu is generally composed of soup, which I particularly appreciate, both for the taste and because it warms me, along with some chicken and fruit. I value the fruit above all because I can save it and eat it during the day, filling the hours a little. At the beginning, a savored cup of tea also serves to interrupt the morning monotony, but it is so strong that in the end I can't drink it: it accentuates the effects of stress and gives me powerful bouts of nausea. It's useless to ask for a weaker cup of tea; only once did they allow me a bit of hot water to dilute it. I don't know if this rigidity is due to circumstances beyond their control, or to their own need to underline my status as a prisoner.

Other discomforts depend entirely on the fact that during my imprisonment I must share with Iraqis the effects of all the damage done by the occupation, starting with the lack of basic goods and services. When I was staying in a hotel, I didn't notice whether the electricity we used depended on public services or a private generator, but I do now. Now I understand the complaints of the Iraqis who repeat *maku karaba* (the power is out) so often that it became a slogan, even written in protest on electoral ballots in the elections of January 30, 2005, to void them. At the beginning, my jailers had given me a lamp and some oil, but now, given that the air in my closed room has become stifling, they light it only when I have to eat. And not always, even then. It's not that the power is always out, but that the allotment is usually no more than three or four hours a day, as I surmise from the lightbulb—I don't control the switch—that illuminates my room. My keepers leave that light on all the time, so after passing almost an entire day in the dark, the lightbulb suddenly blinds me in the middle of the night, interrupting whatever sleep I'd foolishly hoped for, and still only staying on a few hours. To compensate for the lack of *karaba,* my house/prison is equipped with a generator, but even my abductors must deal with the shortage of gasoline, obtainable by now almost exclusively on the black market and for exorbitant prices, and not always available even then. Therefore its use is limited to the evening. Lack of power also means lack of water, which must pass through treatment pumps, and lack of heat, once provided by electric heaters (given energy costs these had become laughable), and now by stinking, malfunctioning kerosene heaters. I suffer terribly from the cold, and I pass my days in bed under a heavy quilt. But when the immobility and the weight loss start to make me dizzy, I decide to dedicate half an hour a day to exercise, because when they finally set me free I want at least to be able to walk straight. And then, I certainly have plenty of time! But it's more than that. Keeping myself in decent physical shape is a way of affirming my dignity.

The life of a hostage, stripped of the possibility of engaging in any activity such as reading or writing, is concentrated for the most part on solving small but crucial problems, such as how to take a shower or cut one's nails. A shower is most often a pipe dream and not only because of the severity of my guards. I can't stand cold water, so in order to take a shower I have to wait for the water to heat, and for that you need at least an hour of continuous electricity. Sometimes, there is actually hot water, but when I finally throw myself under the shower the power goes out and the water dries up in a flash, robbing me of the one relief conceded me every three or four days. The most banal things become a problem, like going to the bathroom more than the two or three times a day allowed by my jailers. So I try to regulate my bodily functions, measuring attentively each night the quantity of herbal tea I can safely drink to correspond to my daily needs and above all to the unforeseeable length of my imprisonment. This herbal tea was the only personal effect I'd been allowed to keep with me. I always carried a packet in my purse against any eventuality (and here I was, in the most wretched of all). Before now, I had never imagined that cutting my nails could become a problem. But after a few weeks of imprisonment, my nails grow too long and begin to break, and I have no way to cut them. My guards leave me nothing that could be interpreted as "dangerous": a lighter, scissors, a knife. For days I have asked, uselessly, for a pair of scissors; then finally one day they allow me a nail clipper, but only for the time strictly necessary.

As for the rest: the void. Twenty-four hours a day alone with myself, with my wandering thoughts, with the terror of losing all contact with reality. I listen intently to all noises. The house where I am being held prisoner must be in an outlying neighborhood of Baghdad. I was brought here without being blindfolded, but I wouldn't be able to recognize it: the city is enormous and my lousy sense of direction is no help. In Baghdad I can barely orient myself on the main streets—Saadun, Rashid Street, etc.—where I've spent the major part of my time. Anyway, wherever I am, I try to reassure myself by imagining my surroundings through noise: the squeak of a passing cart; the cry of a boy selling bread; the voices of kids playing in the streets or in some garden in the afternoon after school; a kitten mewing near my window, or perhaps it's only my imagination that it's so near, because I love cats so much; tires squealing around a curve; a truck horn that passes every morning, making a ruckus; someone banging on the iron gates of the next-door houses, or perhaps of this house, where I'm held. At times my isolation makes it difficult to determine distances.

Friendly sounds and unbearable racket, like the deafening rumble of the generator that goes on for hours, late into the night, drowning out my already agitated thoughts. When it finally shuts down, it's replaced by the deafening roar of the American helicopters that circle above the houses, seeming at times to graze them as if they were intending to land on the roof. Then, if any lights happen to be on, my guards suddenly switch them off. I doubt whether that can help to camouflage us, given the technical gear in the hands of the Americans, which could probably intercept even our conversations. But this doesn't seem to worry my abductors, who, by the way, are always talking on their cell phones. Sometimes I hear the ring of a standard telephone as well, but no one ever answers.

The air traffic at some points is so heavy as to make me think a flight path must pass directly over our heads. When all the racket finally calms down, and I hope to find a little peace in the silence, and even in the dark—which usually increases my sense of claustrophobia—suddenly the bulb above me is blindingly illuminated.

It's not only time that preoccupies me, but the fear of losing my memory. Sometimes at home we would joke about my forgetfulness, but now it's a true obsession. It's not just about counting the days of imprisonment, but about remembering times past. Every morning I promise myself to reconstruct some period of my life. Rummaging around in my memory, starting from the most distant memories of my childhood spent in the Piedmontese Valley of Ossola, in my grandparents' big house; then high school on Lake Maggiore; my university years in Milan, coinciding with the historic protests of 1968; and then political militancy with various leftist groups (both outside the government and then within it) taking me to Rome, and finally leading to my arrival at the newspaper *Il Manifesto* in 1988. And then, traveling all over the world for *Il Manifesto*, following the bloodiest crises: from Somalia to Algeria, from Palestine to Afghanistan, and then Iraq, first in 1990 and then again in 2003. I try to reconstruct my seven trips to Iraq, since I think my abductors may interrogate me on my movements. I try to remember names, places: an exercise to prevent my mind from wandering too freely and falling prey to nightmares. But that's a risk I cannot avoid.

In any event, it's the week that sets the rhythm of my imprisonment. I was abducted on a Friday, a day of rest, and until the following Friday nothing of any relevance happened. I waited for a phantom interrogation they had announced (or threatened) but which never took place. On Saturday morning, with the beginning of the new week, they made me record an excruciating video—the first of two videos which eventually aired in Italy and the U.S., in which I was forced to make a personal plea to my family as well as call on the Italian government to withdraw its troops in exchange for my life. Then another week of waiting, and then on the following Saturday, February 19—the day of the huge antiwar demonstration held on my behalf in Rome—they asked me to write a letter to my family. In it was a section dedicated to my longtime companion and colleague at *Il Manifesto*, Pier Scolari, to be sent along with my watch. It provided the proof that I was alive and fed my hopes for negotiations for the entire following week. And then nothing new until Sunday, when, right after waking, they presented me with a gold necklace. "It's a sign that the negotiations are going well," I thought. And that afternoon, they had me record the second video: "For us, the question is concluded," they told me. And I believed them. The climate in which the new video was filmed was decidedly different: I had to thank my kidnappers for the treatment I received, flanked by two mujahideen armed with Kalashnikovs and Korans. What worried me above all was a proclamation they read at the beginning of the video. I tried to make sense of it, but to no avail; I was too agitated. "Tomorrow or the next day, you'll be heading back to Rome," they told me.

Tomorrow or the next day. What followed instead was the longest week of all. I waited until Friday, when after the last prayer (at 7:30 p.m.) they announced we were leaving. Immediately. It was late: I wasn't expecting it, at least not that day. Just a few hours before I had asked why they still hadn't freed me: "There are still problems to resolve about your transfer," they had answered. Then this sudden announcement. Time underwent an abrupt acceleration, which would immediately slow again during the long wait for my liberators. Then the race toward the airport, blocked by American "friendly fire."

For me, the hands of the clock were suddenly running forward, while for Iraqis, they are continuously turning back.

It was the seventh time I had returned to Baghdad since the beginning of the war in 2003, and every time I found the situation worse than before. Things had deteriorated from all points of view: security, employment, daily life, conditions for women.

For Iraqis, too, time had warped. Making an appointment in Baghdad is risky business. Security problems condition every move on the street—no one wants to go out around 10 a.m., the favored hour of car bombs—and require the use of a car. Children are accompanied right to the classroom door to avoid attacks and abductions. Anyone who has a means of transportation avoids walking, given that you certainly can't count on public transportation.

Under Saddam, it was impossible to import cars freely, so after his fall, the rush to the automobile brought a million new cars to Iraq. The broad streets and highways of Baghdad might have been up to the task of managing this increase in traffic if the principal arteries had not been suddenly shut down by incessant American checkpoints and blockades. In fact, these have provoked enormous traffic tie-ups, fed by drivers who, in the absence of any controls, zoom down the wrong side of the street trying to escape the gridlock. But driving a car also means procuring gas, and those who can't afford to buy it on the black market must spend days and nights in line in front of gas stations, waiting for supplies to be replenished.

Clearly, high unemployment—upward of 80 percent—has also changed the Iraqi way of life. Even marriages have slowed down; it takes too much money to get married: at least two thousand dollars, according to Hussein, my "bodyguard." Conversely, I remember the explosion of weddings on the eve of the war; not only the current one, but the war of 1991 as well. Then, too, I found myself in Baghdad, and the number of weddings surprised me. They were visible everywhere, in the big hotels where the bride and groom spend the first night, accompanied right to the door with a great clamor from relatives, together with singing, drumming bands, and the typical, trilling "youyouyou" of Arab women. Yet even so, beneath all the uproar, there was no euphoria: you realized it the minute you saw the sad expressions on the faces of the bride and groom. Rather, the imminence of war made finding a husband a necessity, to face the emergency. For the more fortunate, even the possibility of leaving the country was tied to a husband. Women were able to skirt the regulations introduced by Saddam in the last years of his regime, when females under forty-five were allowed to travel abroad only when accompanied by a male relative. The urgency of finding a husband in the face of coming war also accelerated the tendency to close oneself off in one's own tribe, raising the number of marriages between blood relatives and consequent genetic illnesses. The new divisions between various communities and ethnicities in Iraq will only accentuate these problems.

The contrast between past and present came up often in my conversations with Iraqis before my abduction. War, repression, and the embargoes had all made life difficult since the 1980s, but with the arrival of the Americans, the situation had further deteriorated. "It was better under Saddam," Iraqis are starting to say, even those who suffered bloody repression. It's not easy to imagine a normal life under a bloodthirsty dictator. Only one thing is for sure: another generation has been lost.

THREE

LIFE-DEATH

BALANCING BETWEEN life and death. Hope and desperation, illusions and disappointment alternate during my imprisonment. Alone with my thoughts twenty-four hours a day, sometimes I fear I'll go crazy. Everything around me I interpret as a message of life or a signal of death; whether real or illusory, it doesn't much matter. I zero in on every sound, every behavior, every glance. And when my thoughts are centered on death, sometimes I have the sensation of becoming untethered from life: suddenly, I no longer feel my body, as though my mind has become disassociated from my flesh. I begin to observe myself from above. It's a sensation that has nothing of the transcendental about it, it's probably a defense: maybe it helps me to beat back death, or simply to escape the dark room where my body is shut up. As the minutes pass, however, the sensation becomes ever more unpleasant, until my freezing feet force me to stir and I begin to recover my physical self, piece by piece. In these moments, even a sheen of sweat, provoked by the mountains of covers I'm wrapped in, reassures me: I'm alive. And I'm still a prisoner, both in body and of my own thoughts, swinging between pessimism and optimism, death and life.

At the beginning the fear of being killed prevails: my guards always have their faces uncovered. This immediately convinces me that they won't let me out alive. "Evidently, they've already decided to kill me, if they don't take precautions," I tell myself. The accusations that follow, that I must be a spy, just reinforce my conviction. Wasn't Enzo Baldoni, the Italian journalist abducted and murdered in August of 2004, slaughtered on just such a pretext? At least that's what they had the two French journalists imprisoned along with him believe. In that regard, how to demonstrate that it isn't true? "They [referring to their leaders] have ways to verify it," maintain my jailers. The affirmation doesn't calm me; if it's true, however, they'll discover that I'm not a spy, and I'll just have to wait. My life is hanging by a thread that any little misunderstanding could break. The wait is maddening: I waited for days for them to come interrogate me, putting my memory to the test in trying to remember every object I had in my purse at the moment of abduction, the telephone numbers, the addresses, the notes, the credentials, and finding for each one a motive, a justification. Then I went over each of my trips to Iraq, all seven of them, starting in February of 2003: where had I been? Baghdad, Basra, Mosul, Nassiriya, Kirkuk, Karbala, Najaf. The images overlap one another, as do the names and faces. I think back to my first arrival in Baghdad, when I lived for more than a month, along with Iraqis, with the hope or the illusion that the war could be avoided. But then, when time was running out on the ultimatum, these people exhausted by war—first against Iran, then the first Gulf War, then thirteen years of embargo—exclaimed in resignation: "If it has to begin, let it begin now, so it will be over quickly." The wait was debilitating, it drained you of all energy. Just like now: "If they have to kill me, just get it over with."

It was also the same time of year. Then, it was the sandstorms that slowed the advance of the troops. Now, if gusts of sand are blowing outside, filling the air with an ocher powder so that you can't even see a few yards ahead of you, I don't know. I can only tell if it's windy outside by the noise of the paper stretched in a wooden frame over an opening in the wall; in the past, the hole must have been used for an air conditioner, now replaced by a bladed fan that hangs from the ceiling. Sometimes, that fluttering, rustling paper is a temptation. I'd like to try to rip it off and see whether the frame crumples: it certainly looks precarious. My abductors must sense my thoughts, and warn me not to touch the covering. Yet even if it concealed a hole big enough to crawl through, I could never have escaped. My guards investigate the smallest noise, even when I open the closet door, never mind the crash of that frame falling! I have no chance. If I even attempted an escape they would immediately catch me—or worse, kill me. I don't think seriously of escape. It's impossible. These thoughts just allow me to mentally evade my prison for a few minutes, to escape the sense of claustrophobia that is strengthened every time the key turns in the lock, underlining once again my isolation from the world. The disappointment is even more bitter on those rare occasions when I doze off and dream of being free in some other part of the world ... waking in prison is terrible! In those moments, my dejection is total. At times, I go so far as to wish that a bomb—from terrorists, from the Americans, it doesn't matter—would tear down the walls that isolate me from the world.

But the worst moments of fear I live through come when the ultimatum set by a group that calls itself simply "the Jihad" runs out. Right after my abduction, the Jihadists had issued a false ultimatum to the Italian prime minister, Silvio Berlusconi: "If you don't announce the withdrawal of troops by Monday, we'll kill her." I hear this on Sunday night, by chance, on a EuroNews broadcast, the only one I am able to see during my imprisonment, aside from the announcement of my abduction on Iraqya TV. In that moment, all my hopes are crushed. My abductors try uselessly to convince me that it was a false claim, that they are not Jihadists, they are not cutthroats, that they have no wish to kill me. After this blow I hole up in my room, and the key turning in the lock in that moment is almost reassuring: nothing will happen till the next night, I console myself.

I have nothing to do but wait. I don't have much hope. I think of Margaret Hassan, a woman my own age, abducted and murdered in November, 2004. She was married to an Iraqi; I had spoken with her husband just a few days before my own abduction, and we were supposed to have met. We didn't make it in time. In a dramatic appeal to the British prime minister, Tony Blair, Margaret had asked for the withdrawal of British troops, to no avail. It would be equally useless to make a similar appeal to Silvio Berlusconi. Margaret was not spared, even though for years she had been actively engaged in the support of the Iraqi people, most recently with the NGO Care International. Why should they behave any differently with me?

Monday night, as the Jihad ultimatum runs out, I try to judge the look on Hussein's face: he seems different, worried, evasive. Perhaps because it will fall to him and Abbas to kill me? And how will they do it? I hope—at least, I convince myself—that as a woman, I'll escape decapitation. They'll use a gun, I think, probably covering it with a pillow to stifle the sound. As if anyone would notice the sound of a pistol shot in Baghdad! The wait is more unbearable than ever. I can't stand it anymore: I knock violently on the door. When my guards arrive, I greet them with a scream: I know you want to kill me, I can read it on your faces! They look at me, dumbfounded: I read their surprise and uncertainty as a confirmation. Since they cannot reassure me, they propose watching television. Maybe it will help calm me. After tidying a bit, they allow me to enter their room, and I curl up in an armchair. The television is tuned to a channel showing an American war movie. I couldn't tell you which one—I see only soldiers, weapons, shooting, images of death that augment even further my sense of anguish. I might as well return to my room and wait. Why are they suddenly being so nice? Perhaps it's only to satisfy my last wish. The last cigarette of the condemned! But here, nobody smokes. Usually my kidnappers get up at 5 am, in time to prepare themselves for prayers at 5:30 (*al fajr*). Sometimes one of them comes to check on me in my room. That Tuesday morning, I hear them both arriving. They open the door with a bang and burst inside. I leap up from the bed. "Here they are, it's time!" I think, resigned. And instead: "Are you awake?" they ask, and then they leave, closing the door noisily behind them. It has been the longest night of my life!

That was not the only time I was afraid they would kill me, but it was the moment in which I most concretely feared that my life was coming to an end. When I think of death, I try to exorcise it by giving meaning to my past life. Day after day as I scroll through my life, I remember friends, companions I'd lost track of over the years…many of them I would see again upon my return, in the photos of the marches calling for my liberation, or through messages and visits. I think in particular of the years of militant pacifism, at the beginning of the 1980s, when the West believed the heart of the problem lay in the Mediterranean, and began accordingly to marshal its most powerful weapons (nuclear missiles) in the south of Italy, at the NATO base in Comiso. For this reason, we Italian pacifists, who were against all missiles, both American and Soviet, wove strong relationships all around the Mediterranean, with Spaniards, Yugoslavs (when there was still a Yugoslavia), Algerians, Greeks. It was a very important period of my life, crucial to my political training and to the maturation of my pacifist conscience. Memories of those years crowd my mind. But above all, I think during my imprisonment of all my companions in those vital political and human experiences who are now gone: Josep Palau, a Spaniard, dead for some years; Sergio from Sarajevo, a victim of a car accident on the road to Hungary during the Balkan war. The most recent wound was the sudden death of Tom Benetollo, president of ARCI (the Italian Association of Recreation and Culture, a fundamental cultural resource for the Italian left). He died in June of 2004 when I was in Baghdad, and since I had no way to share my grief over his passing, I had not really been able to process his loss. Now the memory of these friends suggests the conclusion of a common experience, and in this context, my own possible end finds a place in the continuum, if not a justification, and serves to give some meaning to my death.

Remembering my wanderings around the world brings back all the close calls: at the end of 1992, on the eve of the arrival of foreign troops in Somalia, three colleagues and I had succeeded in reaching Mogadishu from Nairobi in an Italian mercenary's old Cessna, a plane so small and rickety it had to circle around the clouds to avoid disintegrating when it hit turbulence. The airport of the Somali capital was closed because of fighting between various factions; we were the first to land only because the mercenary had good connections with the Somali warlords. Getting to Mogadishu—except when you were traveling with the military—was always a hazard. It was especially tricky when you arrived at the small airport, about fifty kilometers outside the city, which was always busy with shipments of qat, a mild drug that gave rise to a notable amount of business.

It must have been 1996, during the clashes in Kurdistan between the two major parties—the Taliban and the Barzani, now in the government in Baghdad—when I found myself in Shalaklava one night, searching in vain for a ride to Salaidin, where I was expected. No one wanted to take me, because an undeclared curfew was in force. In the end I managed to find a ride, without worrying much about my security. A few years before, in 1991, I was in Haqqari at the Turkish-Iranian border, where Kurdish refugees had fled, escaping Saddam after the first Gulf War. Cholera had broken out and I couldn't even find a place to sleep; in the end, I spent the night in a hovel without closing an eye. And then, there was the incredible accident in Mazar i Sharif (in Afghanistan, in 2002): our car hit a pothole at high speed, blew a tire, and flew off the road in open desert. Fortunately, there were no land mines. After rolling over a few times, the car lay completely crumpled, but the translator, the driver, and I were miraculously safe. And the adventures during the slaughter of the armed Islamic groups in Algeria! Even in Baghdad, I had been abducted before, on April 8, 2003, by a group of Arab fedayeen who believed I was a spy. The intervention of an Iraqi official had saved me. But this bad scare was followed by another: upon my return to the Hotel Palestine, American tank fire hit the floor where I was telling colleagues of my misadventure. I had always downplayed the danger, but I never challenged fate. I always calculated the risks. Now, suddenly, I have a different perspective. It's as if all my lucky breaks have run out.

But can death really have a meaning? All my attempts to exorcise death fall apart when I think about those who love me. About Pier, and my family. So I concentrate instead on messages to leave them, in case my death is decided. My jailers are not such coldhearted killers as to prevent me from leaving these last messages, I think. I have nothing to write on, so I shape them in my memory. I think of my nine-year-old niece, Sofia, with whom I had dreamed of traveling when she grows up. I would write her: "Sofia, I would have liked to have gone on many journeys with you, but unfortunately mine has already ended...." Upon my return, Sofia did not want to speak to me for a long time. Although she hadn't seen the images of my abduction on television, she was deeply shaken, particularly by the journalists besieging us. The minute she heard my name she would retreat to a corner and cry.

I would also have liked to leave instructions to bury me with a peace flag, one given me by my Algerian friend Cherifa with the word *Salaam* in Arabic. Who knew if Pier would remember where I'd put it? Instead, that flag is waving on my terrace right now, a replacement for one I had hung out before the war and which time had reduced to shreds.

Then, suddenly, I rebel against these thoughts of dying: if they kill me, I'll face death when it comes and others will deal with the aftermath. Better to think positively. I try to imagine what I'd do upon my return home: first of all, a vacation. Pier and I had already booked a week's vacation on the Red Sea in March (and if they hadn't shot me right after my liberation, we would have been able to keep our reservations). And then I'd get some cats. I miss my three kitties terribly—all three had died recently, one after another, of old age. They too had been part of my life during the last twenty years. That kitten mewing outside my window keeps me company, yes, but it also spurs a welling of nostalgia for Mizzi, Mozzi, and Saba! There will be other trips, for pleasure and for work. My travels with Pier, during vacations—I try to recall all our destinations during my imprisonment—are always a discovery, a chance to research or verify some aspect of my work. We'll travel again, from Africa to Latin America, by way of the Middle East.

And I'll have a lot to write: about meetings and interviews made in the days before my abduction as well as my imprisonment. Even though it's difficult to imagine, I realize that my life will inevitably be different after this experience. I have had time to reflect on personal relationships, on emotions, on mistakes and priorities. While I swing between extremes of pessimism and optimism, I try to imagine how I might be freed from this prison. I sense that negotiations are under way and my abductors confirm this. They speak of a "businessman," a frequent traveler, who will act as a mediator. But how will these negotiations turn out? I try to read the moods of my jailers to understand: sometimes they're calm, other times they seem nervous. Maybe things are going badly. What are they asking for in order to free me? Money? Too much? Or maybe their goal is political—surely there is a political goal, but is it only political? "In Italy your photos are everywhere. Now you're famous, we've made you famous," Abbas tells me sometimes, with an air of satisfaction. It goes without saying that I would have preferred to remain anonymous, or to be known only for what I write, not as a hostage. Only after my liberation would I come to realize the extent to which this notoriety would change my life.

What is actually happening outside my room? In Italy? I think of the appeal directed to Pier, even though according to Hussein it may not have even been released. The idea calms me—better if they hadn't seen me in that state! But surely they're taking action: beyond the photos, Abbas tells me there are demonstrations ("People in the streets and in the squares: 'Giuliana yes, Berlusconi no,' is his synthesis) but I have no way of knowing the scope. Pier must be working for my liberation, along with my companions at *Il Manifesto*. How hard, I'll discover only upon my return. I assume their lives, too, have been changed. But my dark, closed room limits my imagination.

Abbas is evidently pleased when he tells me about the demonstration, but I've never seen him so enthusiastic as when he comes to tell me that the captains of all the Italian soccer teams have taken the field wearing jerseys that say "Free Giuliana." He's elated. I can't even understand exactly what he's saying, but I gather that the Italian soccer star Francesco Totti played a game in a jersey bearing my name. "Imagine, Totti, Totti himself!" he repeats. For a Roma fan like him, it's the ultimate. I let slip—more as a challenge than out of conviction, since I've never been a fan and I know nothing of soccer—that I'm a Juventus fan instead. Abbas is disappointed but he doesn't stop touting the skill and perfection of his idols. His euphoria is contagious. This is the true globalization: the language of soccer speaks to all, managing to elate even my abductors, overcoming every ideological objection.

The days pass, shaped by the swinging of my moods. Pessimism and optimism give way to each other while I await the results of the negotiations. Just so long as the talks don't break down, I think. After the first video, I write the letter of authentication. Then a message recorded suddenly by Hussein on a cassette, heedless of the fact that my voice cancels out the taped verses of the Koran (usually my jailers don't help in the making of these videos or letters). The message—says a man covered in a white-and-red kaffiyeh and a matching khaki jacket—must be transmitted to Italy by satellite phone. The procedure seems a bit strange to me, but I don't dwell on it. I usually expect any news at the beginning of the week, but oddly, they have me record this phone message on a Friday, respecting the Italian weekend more than the Muslim calendar.

Saturday goes by in the futile wait for some new signal. It arrives, instead, on Sunday morning: as soon as I wake, when they let me out to go to the bathroom, my guards present me with a red velvet case that contains a gold chain. I look at it, dumbfounded. "The businessman sends it to you," says Hussein. "Our leader," adds the other.

Hussein's manner is clearly awkward: he must not be used to giving women jewelry. One day he told me that he wanted to get married, but had to wait because he didn't have the two thousand dollars necessary for the wedding! I honor the gift by putting on the necklace, as they suggest. I see it as a positive sign: "They wouldn't be giving me necklaces if they planned to kill me!" In fact, a few hours later, in the early afternoon, I suddenly hear a flurry of activity in the next room, the sound of clanking metal, which I would later discover to be Kalashnikovs. I'm trying to guess what's happening when someone bursts into my room, and tells me to put on my clothes to record a new video. "For us, the question is settled, we have to tape this conclusive video, then tomorrow or the day after, you'll be off to Rome," they tell me. They start dragging tables and baskets of fruit around, preparing the set for the new recording. I'm confused. I never know whether to believe what they say or if the whole thing is a put-on concocted for my benefit, but in any event I have no choice. I have to follow their orders. They transfer me to another room, where there's more space. They have me comb my hair. This time they go find me a mirror: it's the first time I have seen my own face since the start of my imprisonment. The image I see reflected in the mirror is nothing to boast about, but at least I can see myself: up to now, I'd been forced to stare at the shadow created by the light bulb on the wall to remember what I looked like. I have no time to reflect: "You have to say that we haven't maltreated you, that we have respected you, show the necklace that we gave you" (now I understand the reason for the gift). The whole speech is pronounced sitting behind a little table bearing fruit, drinks, and the velvet necklace case, according to traditional Arab choreography. I would feel reassured if it weren't for the two mujahideen flanking me, gripping their Kalashnikovs in combat uniform. One is also holding the Koran. "Don't worry," they repeat when they see my unease, "tomorrow or the day after you'll be off to Rome." "Really?" I ask, looking into the eyes—the only uncovered part of his body—of the fighter on my right. "Muslims don't lie," he answers in English, with a piercing stare. I don't feel in the least reassured, even less so when it's he who reads the proclamation that begins with the usual invocations to Allah before my performance. I'm so tense that I don't even recognize the scattered words I usually know. I just hear my name pronounced and I fear that instead of my liberation they're setting new conditions for my release. So it's hard for me to stay calm when it's time for them to film me, particularly since they're giving me contradictory directions. When the video is done, there's nothing more to do but wait. My fears are further fed by the request for a new tape to be transmitted by phone. Monday, Hussein enters the room alone and tells me I must tape a message to my family, indicating the date (like the first time), but without telling me—maybe even he doesn't know—what exactly I should say. The request seems strange after the video of the day before. I gather there must have been some interference. I rebel, but then give in, swearing that this is the last time I'll tape a message of this kind, made stealthily and with no explanation. Hussein accepts my conditions hesitantly.

Monday passes, Tuesday passes, but the promise to send me back to Rome doesn't materialize. I'm gripped by pessimism: something must have gone wrong, maybe the negotiations failed, some last-minute incident. I ask my "bodyguard" for news, but his vague responses only increase my fears. Wednesday night, another flurry of activity, lasting until late into the night. Cell phones are ringing. I hear the word *futur*, the dinner that marks the end of fasting during the month of Ramadan. It's not Ramadan now, but maybe something will happen around dinnertime, I think. Nothing. By Friday, I can't stand it anymore. I hear at least one of my guards go out and I imagine he's going to the mosque. It's cold and damp, raining heavily, water is leaking into the room through the frame covered with newspapers. I call

Hussein to tell him but he says to ignore it. When he brings me lunch, however, he seems a little more vivacious than usual. I take advantage: "Are you pleased?" I ask. "*Shuiya, shuiya...*"(kind of, more or less). "Because I'll be leaving, or because I'm staying?" I persist. "I know that you're going, but I don't know when." Then he calls Abbas, who confirms: "There are still some problems about your transfer, due to the Americans, but they'll be resolved." Hours go by. I'm resigned; in any event, I think, nothing will happen today, it's probably already dark. At that moment, instead, my two guards suddenly burst into the room, all dressed up in Western clothes, and Hussein says, shaking my hand with a cocky air, "Congratulations, you're going to Rome." I'm disoriented, I don't believe my ears. I'm suddenly gripped with fear. "We must hurry, get your clothes on," Abbas urges me. In my room there's a constant coming and going. I don't care if they see me while I dress. My tee shirt is still wet, so I keep my pajama jacket on underneath, you can't see it anyway. My purse is returned to me with money, documents, and a pair of sunglasses. My two phones and my digital camera are missing, they tell me, and so are my notes, though they don't mention those. I know full well that this is the most dangerous moment for me, and my abductors know it too. "Are you ready? Are you calm? Are you sure?" they keep asking. "If you're not sure, we'll wait: when we get out, if someone stops us—Iraqi police, an American patrol—they mustn't figure out who you are, otherwise they'll open fire and we'll all be blown to bits." I'm fully aware of the risks. I've been waiting for this moment for a month and now I'm terrified, but the idea of freedom gives me strength. I ask for a burka-like cloak to cover my face—like the ones Simona Pari and Simona Torretta were wearing at the moment of their release—but they don't give me one. They have me put on my sunglasses and they pad them with cotton so I can see nothing. "We promised your family that you'd return home safe and sound, but be careful: the Americans don't want you to return to Italy alive." These were the last words of Abbas; at the time I think it's just anti-American ranting before my release. Then they take me outside and put me in a car. I can't see it because I'm blindfolded; later they'll tell me it's an old wreck, but at that moment I'm oblivious.

I feel as though I'm still suspended between life and death. The trip doesn't take long. The car stops in a puddle: I hear the splash of water and the motor cuts off. My first thought is that we're stuck in the mud, just at the moment of my release! But I'm wrong. This is the meeting place. My abductors get out of the car: "Wait here, they'll come to get you." Around me, men's voices mutter in the distance. I can hear police cars speeding by, but evidently on a distant street. I imagine one of the large ring roads that link the neighborhoods of the capital city—we must be far out on a side street. What's terrifying me most of all is the American helicopter flying overhead: I imagine it turning, rising, and falling, flying off and then coming back. Every time it moves off I hope this is the moment of release, but nothing happens and in the meantime it comes back. And if it lands? Then I'm done for: my abductors, keeping their distance, will blow me to bits. I'm terrified, but I can do nothing but wait. The wait seems an eternity: my perception of time is skewed. One of my abductors returns and tells me: "Another ten minutes." Ten minutes? What can I do in ten minutes? I decide to count, like a child: one minute is sixty seconds. I'll count up to six hundred, slowly, so when I finish someone will have arrived. It doesn't happen. Should I go on? And now a terrible doubt overlays my fear: how will I be able to recognize whoever is coming to get me? What if, instead of Italians, Iraqis from some other group come to take me? It wouldn't be the first time a hostage was ceded by one group to another. Even though my eyes are blindfolded, I can sense a car with headlights pointed at me. I'm afraid they'll discover me, so I crouch against the car seat. I'm all dressed in black, with my black scarf on my head pulled down to my eyes. I hope they won't notice me. Unfortunately, this is exactly what happens: I'm unaware that just at that moment, there are Italian agents searching for me, and when they don't see me, they move off; but then, luckily, they come back. I'm still sunk in my gloomy thoughts when the door opens: "Giuliana, Giuliana. I'm Nicola. I'm a friend of Gabriele and Pier. It's over, you're free. Come, I'm taking you in another car." The voice of Nicola Calipari suddenly chases away all my fears, all my doubts. They've come to free me, I'm certain of it. Still blindfolded, I climb in the car that has come to get me. After a few minutes I take off the cotton wadding covering my eyes, and while I watch Baghdad fade into the distance, I begin, still incredulous, to grasp the idea of regaining my freedom.

I loved Baghdad from the first moment I saw it, in December of 1990. It was very different then, a city of wealth and grandiosity, while now it seems a shadow of its former self. Even during the war and occupation I always hated leaving, however awful the situation; I was always leaving something undone, and I looked forward to a quick return. Not this time. I see the domes of the mosques fade away and I feel only relief.

BAGHDAD FADES AWAY

Relief for me and sorrow for the Iraqis who remain. I made many friends over these last two years: some have already left the country, others are trying to follow. Yet it's not easy to obtain a passport, much less a visa for a Western country. For Iraqis, too, caught between life and death, basic security is the biggest problem. It's a daily nightmare, when they have to go out or send their children to school. Fear of being hit by an exploding car bomb, or finished off by a spray of American machine gun fire because of one wrong move when a military convoy rumbles into the hellish traffic of Baghdad, or simply because you pass in front of a base or a U.S. checkpoint at the wrong time. Fear of being abducted. Kidnappings aren't only a problem for foreigners: thousands of Iraqis are taken hostage, for ransom or extortion. Doctors, university professors, and other professionals have all been abducted in an attempt to force them out of their jobs in a country under occupation. Some of them never return home. Those who work with foreigners are often among the abductees, since they're believed to be "collaborators"; the same goes for government workers, or employees of almost any institution at all. Other Iraqis are kidnapped simply to obtain a ransom, calculated according to the family's means. Naturally, the fee can also be negotiated. Not even the youngest children are spared. A friend told me of an abductor who went back to the parents to ask for a bottle with which to feed their kidnapped baby—only a year old—who was crying desperately. For this reason, children are kept shut up in their houses by their parents. They can no longer play in the streets or yards. I remember one mother who stayed by her daughter's side right through her exams out of fear of abduction—which for girls, even the very young, often means rape.

In Baghdad they had even told me of an "office for the rights of the sequestered," where families could turn to get in touch with the abductors of their loved ones and determine the amount of the ransom. The office gave out cell phones and satellite phones, and police officers were among the accomplices—in some cases sharing in the spoils. An acquaintance of mine told me about a wealthy neighbor's son, who had been abducted and then ransomed for a considerable amount. Yet the boy had recognized the place where he was held, by the voice of the imam broadcast over the loudspeaker of a nearby mosque. When the father turned to the local police to denounce the crime and get his money back, he was told that it was too late, that the loot had already vanished, with the police as accomplices.

In Baghdad, anything can happen with the most complete impunity.

FOUR

WAR

THE ECHOES of war reach me even in my cell: the rumble of the American helicopters that fly low enough to graze the roofs of the houses, or the explosions, usually in the mornings, one hears in the distance. Just the "usual" car bombs, signaling the beginning of the day. Another day of war. When I was still free and staying at the Hotel Palestine, I'd step out on the balcony of my room to search for the site of the explosion, identifiable by the column of smoke rising from the rubble. Once I found the spot, I'd try to get there. It wasn't always possible: rumors would overlap, the news was contradictory, the nearby streets would be blocked off by American soldiers or Iraqi police. Now, instead, I can only imagine the smoke signals; sometimes I ask my abductors for news of the explosions whose echoes reach us, but they always respond vaguely and without comment, much less with any claim of responsibility. Car bombs, attacks on the troops, downed helicopters: my abduction, too, is an act of war.

But why did they seize me, in particular? The question torments me day and night. If they truly want to liberate their country, as they say they do, is it possible they don't see that it would be better to let me do my job? Is it possible that the "resistance"—as my abductors define themselves—doesn't care about documenting the conditions of the refugees in Falluja? When I pose the question, my abductors respond dryly: "This is war." I myself, while denouncing the degeneration of this conflict, had underestimated its perverse effects—I knew enough to fear the possibility of abduction, but I hadn't seen how very possible it was. Put one foot down on Iraqi territory and for all intents and purposes, you're entering a battlefield. I now realize I hadn't taken this into account. What's more, having contact with Iraqis, moving around the city in the course of my work, made me more vulnerable. Why? "People might tell you things you shouldn't know," my abductors say, and "these revelations can put resistance groups at risk." No one wants witnesses: neither the occupiers, who went to war on a pretext built of lies, nor the occupied, who fear any revelations about themselves as they fight the occupation. Information becomes the enemy, another victim of war. Today, in an era when technology allows us to disseminate information in real time, independent news can be dangerous. Therefore, journalists are also potential enemies. The killing of Waleed Khaled, a sound technician for Reuters hit repeatedly by American fire on August 28, 2005, puts the number of journalists killed in Iraq since the beginning of the war (or since March of 2003) at sixty-six. Contrast that with Vietnam, where in twenty years of war, sixty-three members of the press lost their lives. Another Reuters cameraman, Ali Omar Abraham al Mashadani, was arrested in Ramadi on August 8, 2005, and imprisoned at Abu Ghraib without ever being charged. Journalists in the crosshairs, in other words.

Yet the abductors depend on the news that arrives by satellite from the Gulf stations, particularly Al Jazeera and Al Arabiya. No Iraqi trusts the pro-American Al Iraqya station. What's more, armed groups use the Internet to communicate their claims of responsibility, whether true or false. But here I am, locked in a bare room, without so much as a newspaper or a book to read, dreaming of a pen and piece of paper—I don't dare imagine a computer—trying to eavesdrop on any snippet of news I can glean from the next room. The only transmissions I recognize are the unmistakable soccer games that go on every Friday (the Arab teams) and Sunday (the Western teams). Soccer is the one unbreakable bond, able to cross every boundary—political, ideological, religious—and due to my own ignorance of the sport, I'm excluded.

All of this represents a defeat, which I don't dare admit, even to myself. Up until the eve of my last departure I had kept the pressure on: run the risks, go to Iraq, report on the terrible effects of the war. And that's what I had done: in Baghdad, I left the hotel every day, as opposed to the majority of my colleagues. I was on the ground, refusing to be embedded in any army. It was risky, and I knew it. Some of my colleagues, mostly foreigners, had begun to use armed guards as a deterrent, though in some cases it's been precisely these "Iraqi protectors" who sell their charges to the armed groups. It's a war that grows ever more dirty, from all points of view. The U.S. ambassador at the time, John Negroponte, exported to Iraq the Honduran model of using "contractors" for any dirty work the army can't handle, triggering a new rivalry between highly paid and unscrupulous contractors and poorly paid, inexperienced soldiers, who will shoot at anyone (civilians, naturally), just to be on the safe side.

The first accusation my abductors leveled at me was that of being a spy. And they tried to support the accusation with facts: "You were in Nassiriya, you work with Italian agents. Why are you so interested in Falluja? You speak Arabic (someone had mentioned this in a televised interview on Al Jazeera), why didn't you tell us?" It was pointless to explain that I know a little Arabic but am certainly not fluent in the language. After that, they no longer spoke in front of me, fear-ing that I could understand them, or perhaps only to increase my own fear. Then, fortunately, they verified the fact that I was not a spy, which undoubtedly saved my life. Only then did they start to use a little Arabic as a means of communication in our complicated, multilingual discussions: a little English, a few words of French and Arabic accompanied by gestures. With this change in climate—the moods of my abductors were extremely erratic—for a brief period I even manage to have an afternoon exchange with Hussein. He would teach me a few words of Arabic (or better, spoken Iraqi, since it differs from the classical Arabic I had studied) and I would translate them into English. This helped to pass the time and make me feel less isolated. Without the accusation of spying hanging over my head, I felt somewhat calmer, but I was still a hostage being used as a weapon. A pacifist who would never dare touch a weapon, I was transformed into a weapon myself! I recall a time in Algeria, when I was putting together a piece on groups of armed civilians who had organized to defend themselves against Islamic terrorism, and a woman wanted to photograph me gripping her rifle. I didn't dare tell her that I would never have used it; instead, I begged off using the leaden weight of the Kalashnikov as a pretext. Now I'm forced to live under the threat of arms: Hussein has a machine gun and Abbas carries a pistol, although neither has ever threatened me directly.

Hostages are weapons of war, a powerful means of blackmail in an asymmetric conflict like that in Iraq. In two years of occupation, all foreigners have become the enemy; there's no longer any distinction between governments and those who oppose them, between those who hold passports from countries that supported the war and those who don't. At the beginning of the war, these distinctions existed, but not any more; we have all become "Americans" and I, along with other hostages (Florence Aubenas and Hussein were abducted one month before me), am a prisoner of war. And in fact, that's how I'm treated by my abductors, who even respect some of the written "rules" of international conventions, created when no one foresaw the use of abduction to take prisoners. Conventions that the Americans, however, ignore, since in the preventive war of "detainees"—from Guantánamo to Abu Ghraib—they don't even recognize the status of "prisoner of war."

In any case, I refuse to accept the condition of prisoner, and this allows me to be combative, to maintain a level of defiance and confrontation that makes me feel less subjugated. It is a clash born of cultural, political, and religious differences, and as such, is very difficult for my abductors to accept. Even when we begin from some shared principle, logic leads us inevitably to differing conclusions. And those differences are heightened by the conditions in which our confrontation takes place, which paradoxically allow me a glimpse of a world that would otherwise be difficult to access. Unfortunately, at a very high price. Too high.

I feel that I'm a prisoner and victim of a war that I, like millions of others, have always opposed—futilely. And now I feel doubly defeated.

I understand the motivation of those who oppose the occupation but I cannot support their methods: the use of civilians, the killings of other Iraqis, acts condemned by Sunni religious authorities as well. Civilians are the principal victims of modern wars, fought with "smart bombs" that aren't so smart after all. Women and children caught in bombing raids, that's who make up the majority of victims of the American invasion. I think back to Hilla hospital, where I'd gone during the bombing of April 2003; to the wounded—dozens and dozens, on top of the more than sixty dead—heaped up even in the lobby. For the most part, they were children— even babies just a few months old—women, and old people, all hit by cluster bombs, which by their very nature are designed to strike civilians. We're talking about explosive devices that each contain around 200 "bomblets" about the size of a soda can, whose fragments spray out upon exploding, penetrating bodies and provoking internal hemorrhage, often lethal. Those that don't explode right away—around 5 percent—stay on the ground and become dangerous land mines. According to U.S. Central Command, American troops launched 10,782 cluster bombs during the war. As reported by Human Rights Watch, the equivalent of two million bomblets was dropped in Basra, Karbala, Hilla, and the crowded neighborhoods of Baghdad. As I was able to verify at the time both in Hilla and in Baghdad (in the Biladati neighborhood, inhabited mostly by Palestinians), the victims were above all women and children. Again, civilians make up the majority of victims in all modern wars. How many civilian victims has the Iraq war claimed so far? There are no official figures, a telling contrast with the careful tally kept of Western victims. By September of 2005, the number of American soldiers killed in Iraq since the beginning of the war in March 2003 had topped 1,900, along with 14,000 wounded. These are the official figures, but other voices point to much higher numbers (no wonder Bush won't allow television cameras to film the returning coffins). No one counts dead Iraqis; there are no confirmed figures on the victims of the November 2004 attack on Falluja and the estimates diverge widely. According to the Iraq Body Count (IBC), a British organization that publishes daily estimates of victims on its Web site, between March of 2003 and March of 2005, there were 24,865 civilian deaths, of whom more than 4,000 were women and children. These figures, contained in the report "Dossier on Civilian Casualties in Iraq 2003–2005," edited by professor John Sloboda and put together by

Iraq Body Count and the Oxford Research Group, are based on accounts pulled from the Iraqi and international press, citing only verifiable hospital sources and obituaries. One can only assume that the number of "certified" deaths must be lower than the actual total. Furthermore, that figure doesn't take into account the victims of the months following the conclusion of the study, a period which was particularly bloody.

Half of the victims were in Baghdad, where a fifth of the roughly 25 million Iraqis live. One-third were recorded during the invasion—6,215 in the first year of occupation—while in the second year the figure almost doubled, to 11,351. Again, according to Iraq Body Count, 37.3 percent of deaths are attributable to coalition forces (and 98.5 percent of those deaths are by U.S. troop fire), while 35.9 percent are attributable to common criminality. The antioccupation forces and the terrorist groups have increased their activities as time goes on, causing 9.3 percent of civilian deaths. Another 11 percent of victims are attributed in the IBC report to "unknown agents" (like those of the many recent attacks on Shiite mosques). "The IBC has compiled a credible list of deaths using only published press reports and the computer," wrote the British medical journal *The Lancet* in an editorial. But the "net refusal of the U.S. and coalition countries to keep count of Iraqi deaths makes a mockery of the principles of the Geneva Convention, which establishes that invasion forces must make every effort to protect the lives of civilians" (*The Lancet*, July 31, 2005). In October of 2004, the same weekly had published an investigation into the overall number of deceased in the first year of the conflict: deaths had risen by 100,000 over the previous year, of which 40 percent were considered a direct consequence of the war. In its 2005 annual report, the Small Arms Survey, a research group at the Graduate Institute of International Studies in Geneva, also calculated the number of civilian Iraqi victims between March of 2003 and April 2005 to be around 39,000, based on epidemiological research.

There are almost no figures on Iraqi military deaths in the conflict, either: the approximate numbers proposed range from 4,895 to 6,370. The number of wounded is also extremely high; of the 40,000 wounded indicated by Iraq Body Count, many cases have grave complications, adding to the number of disabled created by the country's previous wars.

The violence in Iraq seems destined to increase: the U.S. will continue to try and suppress the guerrillas, and will end up striking mostly civilians, who to defend their own dignity will increasingly take the side of the antioccupation forces—precisely the scenario that played out in Falluja.

"MAKU KARABA" (THE POWER IS OUT)

Hostility toward the occupation also stems from the unbearable conditions in which most of the population is living. Electricity comes and goes, notwithstanding the American-style PR slogans that appear on billboards and on television: "Electricity is a gift, help us protect it." It's a gift above all of Iraqi oil, though it doesn't filter down to the population: *maku karaba* is the most frequently heard phrase on the street. Iraq requires around 15,000 megawatts a day, but it has only 5,000 at its disposal, says Latif Rashid, minister of water resources. The supply of electricity, according to the Americans, is supposed to be guaranteed at least sixteen hours a day in Baghdad, but as I had occasion to witness during my captivity, the power was never on for more than four or five hours at the house where I was held. The Americans have often used cuts in service—electrical, water supply, etc.—as collective punishment in the most rebellious neighborhoods. It could be that I was held in one of these areas, but from what I heard the situation was no better in other quarters. "The demand has risen," maintains the U.S. command, which claims to have increased production by around 232 megawatts. Three additional projects should increase production at the al Dora power plant, which supplies the capital with 428 megawatts, according to U.S. sources.

It would take an investment of 20 billion dollars to restore electrical supply plants throughout the country, claims the Iraqi minister of electricity, Mihsin Shlash. The minister has drawn up an ambitious five-year plan for raising electrical production to 18,000 megawatts in 2010, without, however, providing many details, particularly as regards the financing of the work. In view of the summer emergency, when demand reaches its peak, the minister had asked neighboring countries for help: Syria, Turkey, and Iran provided aid. For now, those who can afford it make up for the lack of power with generators, used by 39 percent of all houses in the capital city. To make them work, however, you need combustible fuel, and there is a shortage of that as well. It's the most absurd paradox in a country afloat in oil, a country which, on paper, boasts the second largest reserves of black gold in the world: one liter of gasoline, which costs twenty dinari (little more than a cent) at the gas station, is sold for five hundred dinari on the black market. What's more, gasoline is imported from Kuwait and Turkey, turning a nice profit for Halliburton, the company formerly headed by U.S. vice president Dick Cheney (from 1995 to 2000), and now accused of inflating costs by more than $3.5 million. That didn't stop the U.S. government from assigning its favorite Texas megacorporation a new contract worth $5 billion, on top of others worth an additional $9.1 billion.

To tackle the scarcity of fuel as winter approaches, a special committee formed by the minister of energy devised a solution: the official rationing of all petroleum products through the use of designated coupons. The rationing includes kerosene, which is used for cooking—given the shortage and high price of propane gas—as well as for heating and generators.

WATER

When there's no power, there's usually no water, at least water pumped through city treatment plants. The bombing ruptured many of the pipes carrying drinkable water, mixing the potable supply with that of the sewers. The first investments have as yet not produced any real changes. The country, crisscrossed by the Tigris and Euphrates rivers, is also fighting a scarcity of water. To restore the water system—badly damaged by war and a lack of maintenance—would take around $15 billion, according to Minister Latif Rashid. "Iraq is a country rich in water resources. We have ample reserves of water, two great rivers, with many tributaries, and a vast marshland," affirmed Rashid during a conference held at the end of June in Amman, "but what Iraq needs is large investments." It would take $10 to $15 billion to repair and construct new dams, irrigation canals, sewage systems, and water treatment plants. The U.S. has allocated $3.7 billion to rebuild the water system, but spending on security absorbs a good part of that sum. The projects financed by the ministry amount to $400 million. The result is dramatic: at the end of June 2005, with temperatures hitting 104 degrees and above, the major part of the capital was without water for a week (according to a friend from Baghdad, who wrote me a desperate e-mail). The authorities put all the blame for the situation on saboteurs. After a week, the water came back on in the neighborhoods of Mansur, Yarmuk, and Khadimya, but not in others, like al Jihad and al Shurta, where at the end of July, with talk of new sabotage at the al

Tarmia plant, there was still no water supply. "Out of desperation, the population of the capital started to drain water directly from the river, reopening old wells, or digging new ones in their yards and gardens, raising grave concerns about health issues," reported the United Nations Integrated Regional Information Network on July 24, 2005. And in fact, when "Talib abu Younes raised a glass of tap water to his lips he saw worms moving on the bottom," reads an article by Leila Fadel, from the Knight Ridder News Service (July 26, 2005). Evidently, it was water pumped directly from the Tigris. The story made me think back to my imprisonment, when I drank nothing but tap water!

"We are forced to draw water from our neighbor's well. We use it for washing and cleaning, but for drinking we buy bottled water, which is expensive," says Haifa Fayyad, a public employee, who lives in the al Jihad district of the capital, where at the end of July there had been no water for more than a month. And there are few who can afford to buy bottled water—in response to demand, the price has risen from fifty cents to seventy-five cents a liter, almost unthinkable for a population still living, for the most part, on government food rations instituted during the embargo. After the war, even these were reduced and distributed sporadically.

Solving this problem will require a lot of time: the capital requires about 16.2 million liters of water per day, but even if all the plants located on the banks of the Tigris were functioning, at best they would provide little more than 10 million liters. And the water shortage doesn't affect only the capital. The authorities justify it by talking of sabotage, which although real, is often used as a pretext to avoid taking responsibility. "In over half the city, where the water problems are worst, there hasn't been a single explosion in the last two years," says Liqaa Maki, an Iraqi researcher. "The fact is that up to now, we haven't seen any real investment in the water system."

Maki cites the example of al Rumaitha, a city north of Baghdad, where "there have been no bombs, no assassinations in the last two years, and where there had never been problems with the water supply in the last decades. But this week the government cut off water to the entire region, giving rise to protests. How can the government blame the resistance when these problems are the obvious result of bad administration and lack of investment?" concludes Maki (www.aljazeera.net, June 28, 2005).

IN THE GARDEN OF EDEN

Some modest investment has been made in the south—$30 million coming from the U.S., Italy, Japan, and Canada, for a job that would require $500 million—to restore the marshes, polluted by the overflowing waters of the Tigris and the Euphrates before the rivers join in the Shatt al Arab, an ecosystem that had been unique in the world for millennia. Here was the place the Bible defined as the "Garden of Eden," and which five thousand years ago saw the birth of Sumerian civilization. Here there are fifteen to twenty thousand square kilometers of marshland, and an immense lagoon dotted by small islands on which 500,000 people lived in reed houses, and where millions of birds once took refuge in the trees during migration. In 1990, almost 60 percent of the Iraqi supply of fish—carp for the most part—came from this area, claims Azzam Alwash, director of the Eden Again Project. Yet by 2002, according to a UN report, the marshes had been reduced to only 7 percent of their original territory. Draining the marshes through the construction of dikes and canals— which also compromised the region's agriculture—was originally the handiwork of Saddam. After the first Gulf War, and particularly after the revolt of the Shiites, Saddam wanted to deprive his enemies (Shiites and communists) of an environment they could hide in, where they became as difficult to catch as fish in water. The neighboring countries of Turkey, Syria, and Iran have helped make the situation worse by constructing dams and diverting water from the two rivers. This scarcity of water now makes it difficult to restore the original habitat. Forty percent of the land has been reflooded, but to restore the natural cycle of water would take careful management, requiring technological skill and financial investment, and above all, a flow of water sufficient to cleanse the earth of salt (which prevents plant growth) and sulfur. Researchers have also discovered abnormally high levels of selenium, a toxic metal that can accumulate in the food chain, gradually poisoning the entire ecosystem.

Industrial pollution further endangers the health of the local population, along with the aftereffects of the bombing raids from both Gulf wars (toxic refuse abandoned by soldiers during the invasion: see *National Geographic*, April 2003), which included the use, among other things, of depleted uranium. The most common effects have been allergies, miscarriages, birth defects, and tumors. Alarm has focused on the high percentage of birth defects, particularly in Basra, as denounced by Suzie Alwash, wife of Eden Again Project director Azzam. Up to now, about forty thousand evacuees have returned to the marshes, while others continue to live in nearby villages or in the cities where they moved or were deported during the marshland draining. Even before the restoration of the ecosystem, these people need immediate aid—clean drinking water and health care above all.

Toxic residues from oil well fires during the first Gulf War present another disastrous environmental problem: according to Jonathan Lash of the World Resources Institute, it will take at least one hundred years to eliminate all the contaminating factors. And then there are the landmines accumulated during the various wars and still un-exploded: between eight and twelve million, according to estimates of the Mines Advisory Group, a UK-based humanitarian organization and leading specialist in mine clearance.

The situation, from the environmental point of view, has deteriorated notably since the invasion of 2003, due to the continued use of ammunition containing depleted uranium, and the looting of dangerous and toxic materials.

"Iraq is the worst case examined so far, difficult to compare with anything else. After the Balkan war, for example, we were able to intervene immediately for the protection of the Danube, but not in Iraq," says Pekka Haavisto, former minister of the environment in Finland and current president of the United Nations Environmental Program Task Force.

AN IRAQI CHERNOBYL

In addition to the environmental damage produced by bombing, there's the damage provoked by toxic materials looted after the invasion, which the occupying forces did nothing to stop. The most striking cases were at the Tuwaitha Center for Nuclear Research and the refinery in al Dora, but there were also the factories making cement and fertilizer—of which Iraq was a principal producer—and various industrial and military complexes. At least five thousand barrels of chemicals, including tetraethyl lead, were burned or hauled away from the warehouses of the al Dora refinery, on the southern outskirts of Baghdad. The effects of the looting of the fifty-six-square-kilometer nuclear complex in Tuwaitha, meanwhile, will only be measurable in years to come. The Tuwaitha Center for Nuclear Research is about forty kilometers south of Baghdad, and it was here that the program for development of an Iraqi nuclear bomb was based. That research was abandoned in 1981, after Israel bombed the most powerful of the reactors, which had been supplied by the French. Two other, smaller reactors remained, one Russian and one French, neither of them able to sustain development of nuclear weapons and bombed, in any case, by the Americans in the first Gulf War of 1991. During the most recent war, however, only two missiles fell on the center, and even those may have been in error. However, the storage warehouse—the so-called "Location C"— did contain radioactive material. American troops were urged to protect this area by Mohammed el Baradei, director of the International Atomic Energy Agency, which had been responsible for monitoring the site before the war. But the urging was in vain. I went to the Tuwaitha Center as soon as word spread of warnings from Iraqi nuclear researchers, at the beginning of June. The day after the arrival of American troops, around three thousand barrels of nuclear components (radioactive waste and enriched uranium) had been looted from the warehouse, while the inhabitants of the nearby village of Ishtar stood by helplessly. Looters had strewn yellow cake on the floor of the warehouse, and worst of all, thinking it was fertilizer, on the fields—with incalculable damages in terms of polluted earth and contaminated underground water tables. What's more, the empty drums were then used to store water—many houses in the nearby village of Wardhia don't have running water—or used for milk collection, given that this is a farming area. Once he realized the extent of the disaster, Khadar al Abbas Hamza, the chief of military operations in the zone, tried to recover the drums, but not only did no one particularly want to give them back, many had already been sold. Not even the attempt to buy them back had much success. People didn't realize the danger because the effects of exposure were not immediately apparent (the major risk of such exposure is cancer, particularly leukemia). A first examination, conducted by Iraqi specialists from the local environment committee, measured very high levels of radioactivity. "The water is contaminated, the houses are contaminated, the animals and even the crops are contaminated," said Thair Ismael Jazim. "We discovered high levels of radioactivity in the beds in these poor huts, in the bathrooms and even the hems of women's dresses," added Hamid al Bahily. After insistent requests, ignored at first by the Americans, the International Atomic Energy Agency was finally able to send its own team to ascertain the extent of the disaster. There were many at the time (including editors of the British daily, the *Times*) who feared the risk of a new Iraqi Chernobyl. Now, the danger has already been forgotten, before the full effects have even been measured.

The effects of the war are beginning to have repercussions even in the United States, not least because of the cost: $5.6 billion a month (that's $204,727 for every U.S. citizen, without counting the $45 billion allocated by Congress so far), an amount higher than the cost of the war in Vietnam. These figures were published in an eighty-four-page report titled "The Iraq Quagmire," by the Institute for Policy Studies and Foreign Policy, at exactly the same time the American public was protesting the White House's delayed response in helping people stranded by Hurricane Katrina. There was a shortage of money and manpower when the hurricane hit. Members of the National Guard who could have helped with rescue efforts were missing, because they had been sent to Iraq. The report, the third edited by this antiwar institute since 2004, contains a plan formulated by Phyllis Bennis for a "complete and immediate withdrawal of troops, military contractors, and American corporations supporting the U.S. occupation." A withdrawal would allow the U.S. to extricate itself from the Iraqi quagmire, but would also let Iraqis choose a different road than that imposed by their occupiers. A clean break is crucial for Iraqis to be able to find a way out of the chaos and terror in which they find themselves enmeshed—although in the immediate aftermath, a withdrawal of troops would certainly not bring peace. Perhaps an internal conflict is inevitable in order to find a way forward—in any case, that conflict is already under way. On the other hand, the governments that contributed to the war and the occupation should identify forms of restitution and humanitarian aid for the Iraqi people that do not consist of rifles and tanks. What the country needs is concrete help in rebuilding, without the theft of its natural resources.

FIVE

RESISTANCE

"WE IRAQIS have the right to fight for the liberation of our country, just as they did in Vietnam, in Algeria...." The new arrival, a mujahideen wearing a dishdasha and a red-and-white kaffiyeh covering his head, begins to recite these words, reading them from a paper gripped tightly in one hand, while the others rush around preparing the "set" for my first video from prison. I can't believe my ears. My rage grows, against the group that has abducted me, but also against myself: it's as though I were being held hostage by my own convictions. I can't even listen to my kidnappers—my two usual "guards" aren't participating in the dramatic performance. I interrupt the mujahideen and yell: "and you're telling *me* you have the right to fight for the liberty of your country? What do you want from me? You had to kidnap me, of all people?" The man—I can see only his eyes behind his glasses—stays calm, unruffled by my reaction, which is perhaps only to be expected. "We know who you are, but this is war. Here we are all at war and we use every means at our disposal. We have to use you as well."

I'm trapped. How will I ever get out of this? Thoughts pile up on each other as they set me on a stool in front of a white wall: there's no banner, no claim of responsibility or identity—maybe they'll add that later, I think to myself. Even if there were a sign, it would be difficult to decipher from the hazy recording (after my liberation I came to find out that they had used the improbable logo of "Mujahideen Without Borders").

For a week I had waited for this moment. From the very first they had said they wanted me to record a video asking for the withdrawal of Italian troops from Iraq, and I had been impatient—might as well do it right away, to see the effect. I had no illusions about its efficacy, but now I realized that I was playing with my life; that an ultimatum could bring me closer to death.

They have me put on my clothes, the ones I was wearing at the moment of abduction. They tell me to fix my hair, but it's not easy: after a week in bed wrapped in my black scarf, my hair is sticking to my head, and I don't even have a mirror. And it's not my physical appearance I want to concentrate on; I don't think of the impact it will have, above all on my family, seeing me appear on the television screen.

I have another goal. My kidnappers define themselves as mujahideen, combatants. Do they truly want the withdrawal of troops? How can they not realize that an ultimatum to Silvio Berlusconi will never get them what they want? Although they're highly politicized, their reasoning leads them to conclusions very different from my own. Anyway, I don't intend to give up the battle: "You can't achieve anything with an ultimatum to the government, and even less with threats to kill me; what's more, I'm a journalist for a small opposition newspaper, who do you think is going to care about me?"

They answer that I must be important because Berlusconi has asked for the intervention of all the Arab countries—even, they emphasize, Saudi Arabia. I'm still not beaten. "If you plan to kill me when the Italian government refuses your demands, better do it right away. After all, it's easier to kill a poor defenseless woman than to go fight the well-armed American troops in the streets." Their response to my provocation is laconic: "We don't want to kill you, we're not cutthroats." So there may exist some margin for mediation, but how to exploit it? How can I avoid sending the classic message: "If you don't withdraw, they'll kill me?" How to make them understand that the same forces in Italy who fought against the war—to no avail, unfortunately—are now opposing the occupation, and anyone who desires the liberation of Iraq should be appealing to the like-minded antiwar movement? But if they kidnapped me, of all people, and are now holding me prisoner, they're certainly not sensitive to pacifist arguments; they're convinced that violence and armed conflict can compel the Americans to withdraw. Yet even if one accepts the option of armed resistance, how do they think they will defeat the U.S. military? Perhaps they can't defeat it, but they can prevent the most powerful army in the world, able to occupy Iraq in just a few days, from controlling the country's territory and resources. And that's no small thing.

The work of the video "technicians" is hindered by the usual power failure and blackout. While they search for an alternative source of light, I manage to convince the abductors that my appeal should be directed not only to Berlusconi and the government, but also to antiwar forces. To make some light during the taping, they find a neon light stamped "made in China"—like almost all household appliances sold in Iraq—that turns my black sweatshirt to green, giving rise to much speculation in Italy about my color choices: Islamic green, military green, or what? No, simply one of the many consequences of chronic power outages in occupied Iraq.

With the installation, however precarious, of the neon light, they can start the taping. Although the meaning of my message is obviously dictated by my abductors—who do not, however, hold me at gunpoint this time—I can choose my own words, though in a language that is neither mine nor theirs. Given a choice between English and French, I choose the latter. This casual choice of French had also created speculation about presumptive ties between my abduction and that of the French journalist Florence Aubenas. But the tone of my appeal doesn't satisfy them: "It sounds like you're reciting a school assignment, you have to be more convincing." They want me to dramatize. Maybe this is why they force me to address my family, and in particular, my companion, Pier Scolari: "Only he can save you, but you have to be convincing. You have to tell him to publicize everything you've done, to show your photos." They've obviously informed themselves about his job as the head of a small advertising agency. And when I address him, calling him by name is not enough, I must call him "my husband," a term I never use. Maybe they doubt I even have a husband, given that no one on television has mentioned that I'm married (because I'm not). Hence, an overwhelming emotion makes up for my lack of conviction. Anyone who saw the video in which I was reduced to tears, witnessed the result.

To tell the truth, they hardly seemed like video experts. In fact, when I asked my bodyguard if the video had been transmitted to Al Jazeera, he answered that the satellite wasn't working right then, so they couldn't see the Gulf television stations, but that in any case, the tape had come out badly so maybe they wouldn't even use it. That possibility reassured me; at least my family wouldn't have to see me in those conditions!

The battle over the videotaping was in some ways my first act of resistance against those defining themselves as mujahideen of the Iraqi resistance. From that moment on, resistance became an imperative. Resistance in order to oppose my abductors; resistance so I would not be brutalized, or reduced to a helpless victim; resistance so as to salvage my dignity. Yet how to resist? I thought of those who had lived through experiences similar to mine, or far more terrible: years of prison, decades of isolation. For me, the symbol of dignity had always been Nelson Mandela; I still remember how he emerged apparently unscathed from twenty-seven years of hard time in an apartheid prison, rising to his appointment with history with perfect grace. The portrait of Nelson Mandela was always before me, only I could see it, no one could touch it. It was like an icon framed on the white wall in front of the bed. Naturally, there was no possible comparison between my imprisonment and his, but his strength illuminated my dark room. Moreover, I was convinced that if I resisted from inside my prison, on the outside the mobilization for my liberation would be even stronger, as if the two were connected telepathically. Something of the sort must have happened—it had nothing to do with the supernatural, but simply with the strength of conviction I shared over the years with my comrades, both those well-known to me, and those I had never met.

Sunday night, two days after my abduction, in a rare moment of flexibility on the part of my jailers—which became ever rarer with the passing of the days—I was able to see a report about myself on an English edition of a EuroNews broadcast. My hopes were not unfounded: the day after my abduction, supporters held a candlelight vigil at the Campidoglio (the capital buildings in Rome), where my photo had now been substituted for those of Simona Torretta, Simona Pari, Manhaz, and Ra'ad (the last two are Iraqi aid workers abducted along with us). To mine would be added those of Florence Aubenas and Hussein Hanoun. There were lots of people, and a close-up revealed the two Simonas as well, standing quietly in a corner. They understood what it must be like for me, more than most; there are some experiences that are hard to convey to others. But my sudden optimism evaporated at the conclusion of the report. "The Jihad" had claimed responsibility, and issued an ultimatum to Berlusconi: if you don't announce the withdrawal of troops by Monday night (it was already Sunday night), we'll kill her. First incredulity, then discouragement, then anguish set in. For the first time, someone had uttered a threat to kill me, and even set a deadline. When my guards realized, perhaps from my reaction, what the televised ultimatum had said, they tried to reassure me, maintaining that they were not part of the Jihad. But as I said, their efforts did little to calm me.

THE ABDUCTORS

Who were my abductors? If it weren't for my fear of being killed, my captivity might even have been bearable. Because in my moments of optimism, I believed my abduction could be a good opportunity to verify "from the inside" all the analyses I had spun up till then on the resistance. But it wasn't easy. Right from the beginning, my principle concern was to figure out who my abductors were: I had discarded the possibility that they were common criminals. My jailers told me they were not al Zarqawi's "cutthroats"; I didn't believe their affirmations, although sometimes I needed to in order to bear those dark days. But then, the exchange or clash of opinions we regularly had led me to believe that they actually were part of that vague cluster of groups that called themselves the "Iraqi resistance." Fear prevented me, however, from asking too many questions, and so I limited myself to observing and listening in order to penetrate the various smokescreens they tried to use to confuse me. It was only at the end that I could draw some conclusions. I admit that at times it was a huge effort to rein in my curiosity, particularly when they provoked me, explaining the distinctions between combatants (mujahideen, trained fighters), and supporters (like my "bodyguard"). They also told me that they were organized in small cells (around ten people) by neighborhood. This was later confirmed by other sources as well. One time Abbas even asked me if I wanted to photograph the mujahideen; I got out of it by reminding him that they themselves had seized my camera.

The mujahideen have deep and branching roots throughout the country, due to their ties to the well-organized Baath Party under Saddam, allowing them to move on the ground with the ease of fish in water. Moreover, it is now commonly held that preparation for armed resistance began even before the Bush intervention. Saddam's threats to the Americans shortly before the war have often come back to me in these months: "We'll let them get to the gates of Baghdad and then we'll fight them street by street, house by house." Drawing from history, as the dictator loved to do, Saddam dubbed Bush "the new Mongol leader," comparing him to Hulago, whose hordes had invaded Mesopotamia eight centuries before. "With the help of Allah I will stop the Mongols at the gates of Baghdad. As he did before, so this new Hulago wants to attack and destroy us," he thundered. The Mongols were not stopped. But "for the Americans, it wasn't a cakewalk, like they wanted their soldiers to believe," Saddam said later: the only prediction the dictator got right.

Scott Ritter, the controversial inspector for UNSCOM from 1991 to 1998, also witnessed "preventive" preparations for a guerilla insurgency to be unleashed after the invasion. Referring to his inspections, Ritter (who the Iraqis accused of being a spy, and who in turn accused Washington of trying to infiltrate the ranks of inspectors) wrote: "While I discovered no evidence of weapons of mass destruction, I found an organization specialized in the construction and use of "improvised explosive devices," the same devices that are now killing Americans daily in Iraq" (*Christian Science Monitor*, November 10, 2003). The organization Ritter refers to is M-21, the special operations branch of Iraqi intelligence. That the guerilla movement has a well-organized, well-prepared component is confirmed by many sources and testimony reported in the press, from local papers like the short-lived *Iraq Today*, to international papers like the *New York Times*. At the same time, the disintegration of Saddam's powerful army and security forces, right after the arrival of the Americans, set free around four hundred thousand unemployed, well-trained, and well-armed Iraqis. The regime's stockpile of arms, in fact, was not immediately dismantled or placed under U.S. control and was thus thoroughly looted. Arms are the only goods in plentiful supply in Iraq. Many ex-military men I spoke to in the summer of 2003 said (maybe to save face) that they were in the military to defend their country, not Saddam; now, given the terrible humiliation inflicted upon them by the Americans, it's not difficult to imagine whom they've turned their arms on. So there definitely exists an organized nucleus of guerrillas, made up essentially of ex-Baath Party members (the party had its own militia) and ex-military men. It's no coincidence that the stronghold of the resistance is in precisely those areas that produced the most officers for Saddam's army: Baquba, Falluja, Samarra, etc. To this nucleus, other forces have been added: tribal, Islamic, and nationalist. Traveling between Falluja, Baquba, and Balad, when it was still possible to get around in Iraq, I talked to many people—young and old—who, while not declaring themselves part of the resistance, supported or sympathized with its aims, and said they were ready to help the mujahideen. Some of the older men—among them a communications engineer purged by Saddam—dreamed of being able to return to the Baath Party's roots, as a nationalist, secular, socialist movement, after the fall of the regime which had so distorted its ideals. Others supported the resistance as a means to avenge the humiliation they suffered under the occupation, or to protect a conservative society from Western invasion. Still others were acting in the name of Islam, which had become a bond in the power vacuum, or even out of simple desperation: a woman whose son—the sole support of her family—had just been killed by the Americans because he happened to be passing by a search-in-progress on the outskirts of Baghdad, told me: "I'm with the resistance with all my heart." Aside from the armed resistance, there is in fact a quiet, passive resistance, made up of small daily acts that get no visibility, and since they don't involve weapons, attract no attention.

In addition, the fact that the armed resistance has no recognized political representation makes it difficult to define its character. The various groups that oppose the occupation cover a vast spectrum and differ widely from one another, on both the political level and the strategies and methods of combat—methods which verge, in some cases, on the margins of terrorism.

MUJAHIDEEN AND JIHADISTS

The liberation of Iraq from foreign occupation is the boundary line that substantially distinguishes the mujahideen and the insurgents from the jihadists, who have transformed Iraq after the American takeover into a theater of war for their jihad against the West. This action is rooted in their vision of a "global Islam": fighting the unbelievers, the infidels, wherever they are to be found. The war, and the chaos it creates, offers them fertile ground. The "jihadists" who come from Arab and Muslim countries, have often spent some time in Afghanistan and they enter Iraq freely, given that the frontiers, after the fall of the regime, remain completely unguarded for long periods of time. They differ from the resistance in their style of fighting and their goals. The culture of death that motivates the suicide bombers is not part of the Iraqi tradition, although the fedayeen, the paramilitary force led by Saddam's son Uday, included a group of members willing to commit suicide. In the marches I saw on the eve of the war, they were marked by their white uniforms, while everyone else wore black. And during the war, on March 30, 2003, as it became clear that it would be impossible to stop the advancing American troops, a noncommissioned officer in the army, Ali Hammad al Namani, blew himself up in a car packed with explosives in front of an American roadblock, killing four marines and wounding many more. This first suicide bomber in Iraq was decorated with highest military honors—the *Um al Marik* ("mother of all battles") medal—by the dictator himself, Saddam Hussein. Ali "the martyr" opened the doors to jihad in Iraq—although, as I remember, in those days the true hero for Iraqis was another Ali, a Karbala farmer who shot down an American Apache helicopter with his hunting rifle. Reality, or popular myth? It didn't matter; Ali served to raise a morale that had been deeply undermined by the sensation of impotence in the face of the unstoppable advance of invaders. Impotence was also the reigning emotion for supporters of a regime in disarray; after welcoming hundreds of "human shields," from many Western countries, and using them to protect strategic points—aqueducts, refineries, power plants—the regime now took aim with kamikaze strikes. In those days (the end of March 2003) then vice president Taha Yassin Ramadhan sanctioned the jihad, the holy war, as a duty "prescribed by God" for every Muslim, and threatened to deploy four thousand suicide bombers from Arab countries. But the explosions would begin only when Ramadhan and Saddam were already out of the picture.

If the suicide bombers are predominantly Arab and not Iraqi, the victims of suicide actions—the favored tactic of terrorist organizations—*are* instead largely Iraqi. In some cases, Iraqi victims are "guilty" of wanting to enlist in the army or the police; in others, they are guilty only of being in the wrong place at the wrong time. Undoubtedly, the creation of an army able to exert territorial control represents a crucial milestone for the future of Iraq. Among the aspiring recruits I had interviewed in November of 2003, many told me of wanting to commit to the police or the army in order to have territorial control in Iraqi hands, an indispensable condition for regaining sovereignty and then asking for the withdrawal of foreign troops. These days, recruits who think they can win back territorial control are probably guilty of naïveté, or are simply searching for a patriotic motive to justify the choice to join the police or the military, in effect one of the few alternatives to unemployment. That naïveté, however, doesn't take into account the interests of those countries conducting the war, who will not easily abandon Iraqi resources. In any case, the presence of an effective Iraqi army on the ground would constitute a huge obstacle for the jihadists, who make Iraqi recruits (considered collaborators) one of their prime targets. The massacre of Iraqis by those who, rightly or wrongly, were identified with the resistance soon created a situation so untenable that the Council of the Ulema (the informal organization of Sunni clergy) was forced to intervene. On Friday, June 25, 2004, during prayers, the condemnation rang out unanimously in all the Sunni mosques, from al Qora (the ex-Um al Mark, seat of the Council of the Ulema) all the way to Abu Hanifa, where I happened to be that day. The mosque of Abu Hanifa, in the heart of the Sunni quarter of

Adhamiya, whose splendid minaret was targeted by mortar fire in April of 2003, was where the Americans believed Saddam was hiding out. The sacred site is a point of reference for the mujahideen. "No one has the right to kill another Iraqi, even if he is a policeman. These killings pollute the image of the resistance," the ulemas had thundered, and that "thought of the day" was instantly absorbed and shared by the faithful I interviewed after prayers. Some were against the killing of Americans as well, others instead felt it was a necessary evil, but killing other Iraqis? No, they said, it had never happened, it was against Islam. The next step from the ulemas was to condemn abductions, the new weapon of war. The condemnation arrived, however, only when the goal of the abductors became humanitarian workers and journalists. For contractors it was different, no one took any position. Contractors are the beneficiaries of the privatization of war: they deal with security and do the dirty work for the occupying forces or the multinational corporations.

If the goal of the resistance is clear—put an end to the occupation and regain sovereignty—it's not clear what the future holds for the country. There is no recognized political representation for the armed Sunni resistance, a nebulous group that includes, as discussed earlier, ex-Baathists, Islamists, nationalists, and tribal leaders, none of whom have as yet found a representative figure to reflect their views. This may be because they are still crushed by the weight of the authoritarian regimes of the past and by the image of Saddam, an icon of sorts. (His image even made a reappearance during the demonstrations against the constitution, although probably not even the ex-Saddamists are still hoping for a return of the ex-dictator). This absence of political representation for militant Sunnis is a weakness not only of the resistance, but also of the whole Sunni community, which finds itself trapped by an armed resistance imposing its own choices. The Sunnis thus end up gaining visibility only through the Council of the Ulema, a recognized religious authority, but without the clout of the Shiite *marjayia* led by the Grand Ayatollah Ali al Sistani (since the Sunnis have no hierarchy of clerics, as do the Shiites). The Sunni religious body has often assumed a stand-in role in relations with the authorities and in politics, but it certainly can't make up for the general vacuum of political representation. Hareth al Dhari, secretary of the Association of the Ulema, explains the position of the religious sheikhs like this: "The resistance is a reality that can't be ignored: it is recognized by friends and enemies. Beyond that, resistance is a legitimate right for any people struck by disasters like those that have struck the Iraqi people. Since we are part of the people and we have influence over them, we support the resistance with conviction. We support the resistance through prayer, and by providing justification [for their actions], while we are under occupation. We are not the leaders of the resistance, nor do we participate in or finance their actions" (interview with Al Majd TV, August 28, 2005).

THE NEW TALIBAN

On a military level, the resistance—although well armed and well trained—certainly cannot compete with the American army, which in turn is not able to defeat a guerilla movement operating on home territory, where it enjoys the support and complicity of the community. Repression, bombings, torture, and discrimination only feed support for the resistance—which, it must be added, is not always voluntary. The armed groups do not shy away from the use of force and coercion. For example, in the elections of January 30, 2005, many were punished for having disobeyed instructions to boycott the polling places by having their thumbs—marked with indelible ink, the distinctive sign of those who had voted—cut off. Likewise, two Sunni politicians were assassinated for taking part in the commission working on the constitution. The execution of spies, or suspected spies, is daily business, as is the imposition of Islamic law by the Wahhabist groups inspired by the Taliban.

The American offensive in the Sunni Triangle failed substantially on the military level: armed groups continue to strike, even in destroyed Falluja, with ever more sophisticated arms and with ever more carefully targeted goals. The carpet bombings penalize only the population, while the combatants easily pick up and move to another area.

The groups tied to Al Qaeda also escaped the attacks. Before the war, only one group existed with definite ties to Osama bin Laden's terrorist organization: Jund al Islam (Soldiers of Islam), founded in 2001 by a union of diverse Sunni fundamentalist groups, one of which was rooted in the Islamic movement of Kurdistan. Some hundred or so members, trained for the most part in Afghanistan, installed themselves in the area around Halabja (where Saddam had gassed five thousand people in 1988) in Kurdistan, on the border with Iran. Here, they took control of a few villages and experimented with a political model based on the caliphate, imposing a Taliban-style life on the population: schools for girls were burned, women not wearing a burka were killed in the streets. And then came war against the Patriotic Union of Kurdistan under Jalal Talabani, which controlled the area at that time. The group had no ties to Saddam, according to its emir, Mullah Krekar, a Kurd who lives in Norway. "As a Kurd, I believe he is our enemy, and also as an orthodox Muslim, I believe that Saddam Hussein and his group are outside the borders of Islam," Krekar had declared in an interview conducted in Norway with the BBC, on January 31, 2003. According to Washington, the dictator had actually financed the group, which since 2003 had assumed the name Ansar al Islam. For Bush, this was proof of a tie between Saddam and terrorism. Thus, at the beginning of the invasion, the Americans, along with the *peshmerga* (the Kurdish separatist militia) of Jalal Talabani, had bombed the Ansar al Islam bases in Kurdistan, forcing the organization to relocate further south in the Sunni areas of Tikrit and Mosul. Among the actions openly claimed by the group, now operating under the name Ansar al Sunna (according to some, this was a simple name change, while others maintain it is a splinter group of Ansar al Islam), were the suicide attempts against the seats of the two major Kurdish parties on February 1, 2004, in Erbil (more than one hundred dead) and the attack on the canteen at the American base in Mosul on December 21, 2004 (more than twenty dead). And then there have been various abductions and the murder of hostages. The most important discovery was made by the British daily, the *Guardian* (August 22, 2005): In collaboration with the Tawhid group, headed by Abu Musab al Zarqawi, Ansar al Sunna controls the little agricultural town of Haditha, two hundred kilometers northwest of Baghdad, on the banks of the Euphrates. Here, the Wahhabists are trying out their caliphate: alcohol and music are forbidden, women are veiled, relations between the sexes are tightly controlled, and adulterers are whipped. Even the cellular network has been blocked. In any case, the mujahideen—as they want to be called, even here—use walkie-talkies and satellite phones, while the right side of every street in the city is reserved for their cars. Decapitations take place at dawn on the Haqlania bridge, at the entrance to Haditha. Anyone who can't watch the event in person can find a DVD with a taped version that same afternoon at the market. The article in the British paper calls it a Taliban mini-state, built under the nose of the Americans, who just one year ago were boasting of having been able, with the Army Corps of Engineers, to overhaul the workings of a nearby power plant and deliver twenty-four-hour-a-day electricity to this town of ninety thousand people (probably the only place in Iraq with such service). Now it's the mujahideen who profit from this success, the militants of Ansar al Sunna who have claimed the right to decide who lives and who dies in Haditha, how inhabitants must dress, and what they can see and hear. Until a year ago, the town was one of many in Anbar Province, in the heart of the Sunni Triangle, periodically at the center of clashes between insurgents and American troops. But now the terrorists have adopted a new tactic: when the American air strikes arrive, they take off, abandoning the populace under the bombs, and as soon as the planes are gone they come back. They don't want to meet the same end as the fighters in Falluja. In fact, it is civilians who yet again are the primary victims of the attacks on Haditha, just as in nearby Rawa and Parwana. Doctors there are appealing for help in fighting a true humanitarian crisis: hospitals are facing shortages of antibiotics, oxygen, and other basic medicines. But for the militants of Ansar al Sunna, it's not worth the effort to lose men in clashes with foreign troops. Beyond the U.S forces, these militants must fight the "apostate" Shiites now in government, says al Zarqawi, who (legend has it) visited Haditha for a few days in mid-August of 2005.

The local tribal leaders are afraid of the terrorists and so they don't rebel, out of a desire to keep "order," which the fundamentalists enforce with strokes of the whip and decapitations—exactly like the Taliban in Afghanistan until a few years ago. Is this the "Afghan model" the United States wanted to propose in Iraq, with its transfer to Baghdad of Afghan American Zalmay Khalilzad, former ambassador to Kabul and a neoconservative favorite of Bush? Instead of eliminating terrorism, they are generating the perfect conditions for its spread.

SIX

RELIGION

"I AM Abbas, and he is Hussein." That's how my two jailers introduced themselves as soon as the other two abductors had gone, leaving us in the house that would be my prison for four weeks. Abbas
and Hussein are the names of two imams, sons of Ali, the founder of
the Shiites, to whom two splendid mosques are dedicated in the sacred Shiite city of Karbala. There are two enormous sanctuaries
dominated by golden minarets and domes, built one in front of the
other, separated only by a broad avenue, constantly crowded with
pilgrims from Iran. Maybe my jailers wanted me to believe they were
Shiites, or perhaps they were just playing with me. Like when we
spoke of Ashura, the days of mourning that celebrate the martyr-
dom of Hussein and Ali with a grim ritual: men flagellate themselves
with metal chains, covering themselves with blood, at times losing
consciousness or even dying. Under Saddam the ritual was forbidden, but after his fall it was taken up again, with increased fanati-
cism. This year, the celebration of the tenth day of the month of
Muharram, according to the Hejira, fell precisely during the period
of my imprisonment. Abbas wanted to make me believe that he was
going to Najaf (the most sacred city for Shiites, where the tomb of
Ali is located) for Ashura. "Want to come?" he asked. As though it

had been a serious proposal, I answered that the ritual didn't fill me with enthusiasm and I had absolutely no desire to watch the useless spilling of blood. To tell the truth, he too was wearing a look of disdain, whether for the ritual or for Shiites in general I don't know.

In any case, given the names they chose for themselves, as soon as I begin to recover from the shock of the abduction, I nicknamed Abbas and Hussein "the Karbalites." I planned to name the first newcomer Ali, without waiting for introductions. I could play this game, too.

Beyond names (I learned after my liberation that Sunni abductors often use Shiite "battle" names), I never had any doubt that they were Iraqi and Sunni (aside from everything else, the Shiites, so far, have not used kidnapping as a tactic). This was important information, although it did not exclude the possibility that they belonged to some terrorist group that was part of al Zarqawi's network. Abbas and Hussein were only guards, but clearly more than manual laborers. They had studied—one said his university studies had been interrupted by the arrival of the Americans—and they were politicized. Apart from pretending to be Shiites, without great success or much conviction, they also wanted me to believe they were very religious, but they never defined themselves as either Salafists or Wahhabists (the most fundamentalist strains of Islam, with the most rigorous vision of the faith), as had the abductors in other cases I was familiar with. As soon as we arrived in the house/prison we were supplied with food, and Hussein (he seemed the most interested) was also equipped with a tape player and recorded verses of the Koran. Both of them got up at five o'clock every morning to pray, but while Hussein wandered around all afternoon with the tape player, spewing out Koranic verses for hours, Abbas seemed to prefer soccer games and movies on television. It was hard to tell whether the afternoon litany was a cover or a religious practice born of conviction. Tradition and religious conviction were often confused in their behavior. My "other-ness," as a Western woman who travels around the world alone, albeit for work, surprised and intrigued them: "You mean your husband lets you travel around alone?" Sometimes, I was able to sense their curiosity, when they allowed themselves a little time at night to talk to me: Hussein knew a bit of English, Abbas knew a few words of French, I used the little Arabic I knew, and we filled in the missing words with gestures. In truth, I felt a bit like a monkey at the zoo, but the curiosity was reciprocal and I took advantage of the situation to try and find out more about them.

At the start of my imprisonment they asked my age: fifty-six. Are you married? Yes. I certainly couldn't explain that I'd been living with my companion for twenty-five years. How old is he? Fifty-three. Fifty-three? He's younger than you! But the thing they found the most unsettling was that I had no children. "And your husband hasn't left you? Does he have another wife?" It was no use explaining that for us, having children is a choice; it would be too complicated, and I didn't want to underline our differences more than necessary. But the idea bothered them, it gnawed at their convictions, and after a few days one of them came to ask me, with much discretion, if I had ever consulted a doctor to seek help for my supposed "infertility." I must admit that my wit occasionally failed me, and I didn't have the presence of mind to venture the idea that the infertility might not be on my end. That would certainly have shaken them up.

At the moments when I would protest the length of my imprisonment, they would jokingly respond that I'd be better off staying in Iraq, since I could always find a husband (in this case they hadn't taken into account the incompatibility between my age and local tastes). When I would answer that one husband was plenty, thank you, they would tease me: "Why, do you think he's still waiting for you? In the meantime he'll surely have already found another woman." Macho clichés don't differ much between East and West. At that point, I was unaware of everything Pier was doing for me. I would discover the extent of his efforts only upon my return, but in any case, it was far more than I could ever have imagined.

Contrary to what other women hostages have experienced, I was never veiled during my captivity, nor did my jailers ask me to cover myself. When I recorded the videos, they always had me wear my own clothes; apparently they wanted me to look like myself. Thus, when I put my black shawl over my head it was only because I was cold. But in the brief exchanges/clashes of ideas I would have with my guards, the question would always arise: "Why don't you convert to Islam?" Sometimes, in truth, it seemed less like a question and more like a way of making conversation, which would then slide inevitably toward the query: "But is it true that you're *shiyooi* [a communist]?" I pretended to ignore the significance of that word, but I knew full well that they had heard it on television, every time news reports spoke of me or my newspaper, *Il Manifesto*, "a communist daily." I tried to avoid answering because I didn't know what was worse to them: being Christian or being a communist. Almost certainly, communists were worse: under Saddam, Christians had freedom of worship, although they were not allowed to proselytize, while communists were physically eliminated. Did they think the same way? I had no way of knowing, but their insistence on the issue made me suspicious. To get a response, they tried to back me into a corner, pulling out the example of Fidel Castro, while I diverted the argument toward Guantánamo and issues of torture in the prisons where Taliban fighters and suspected terrorists were held. In fact, it was at Guantánamo that the prison warden, General Geoffrey Miller, had first experimented with the forms of torture he later exported to Abu Ghraib.

In the end, when I couldn't escape their insistence—"you're *shiy-*

ooi, you're *shiyooi*"—I tried to explain that one could be communist and Christian, or communist and Muslim. But Hussein, breaking his usual reserve, pronounced: "No, communists are godless." This made me reflect: I was effectively, "without God." During my imprisonment, I thought at times of friends who were atheists, like me, but who then, in the face of a particularly difficult situation or terrible loss, had felt the need to seek some transcendental point of reference. Despite the difficulties, the risk of being killed, I never felt the need to pray, to find a God I could turn to; my obsession, instead, was to keep myself tethered to earthly reality. Yet when I got home, among the people who suffered over my kidnapping and worked for my freedom, there were many who told me that they sought comfort and hope in prayer. "We prayed for you," I heard all the time. While I thought to myself that if I hadn't found faith in the midst of such dramatic circumstances, I probably never would. Who knows?

So this was the background when one night—perhaps to confirm my own convictions or to dispel my image as an unbeliever—I gave in to the pressure of my jailers: I recited a prayer from the Koran, repeating the words after them. At the beginning they assumed the position of the Sunni faithful—which is different from the Shiites—during the prayer, and when I mentioned this, they seemed to appreciate my knowledge. That time they did have me cover my head with my black shawl to pray. But to be a good Muslim, they added at the end of the recitation, I should have covered my face as well, leaving only the eyes uncovered, like the Wahhabist women. Exactly like the Fallujan refugees who covered their entire bodies to please Sheikh Hussein. Given my rebellious nature, however, they had concluded that even such modest fashions would not make me more submissive, as religious fundamentalists would like Muslim women to be; on the contrary, according to Abbas, I'd be better off in the clothes of a fighter: the mujahideen also hide beneath a kaffiyeh or a black cloth.

I was able to dissuade them from photographing me in Islamic costume by arguing that religion is a serious thing, and not something to manipulate. I was fearful, naturally, of the use they might make of such a photo (I was always distrustful of their motives, and I had every reason to be).

Imprisonment made the religious cloak my abductors wore seem even more oppressive, perhaps because it added to my claustrophobia. Abbas and Hussein might have wanted to underline my status as a prisoner this way, although it never turned into outright subjection: I was always able to be combative, ready for a confrontation. Even when they told me that a woman cannot speak in the corridor or must not knock too loud on the door, I retorted by simply raising my voice. Sometimes I'd knock and they'd take their time, or they'd bring me a cold dinner because—this was my impression—they had to finish their own meal first, an attitude displayed above all when they had guests, whom I could only hear rather than see. I don't know if this treatment was part of the prison rules, or if the jailers made it a point of honor, or if it had to do with my being a woman or simply a prisoner. At these times they reminded me of the Taliban. My anger would grow—I would have loved a pair of high-heeled shoes to provoke them with, but unfortunately they'd only given me a pair of plastic flip-flops. In Afghanistan, in fact, under the rule of Mullah Omar, high heels were forbidden: their noise would have been an irresistible siren song for men! That's why one of my wishes during those days of captivity was—if I ever got out alive—to put on a pair of red high-heeled shoes I'd once bought in a moment of New Year's folly and would probably never have worn again, had they not become a kind of fantasy during my imprisonment.

Despite all this, my guards were far from those Taliban militiamen—"for the prevention of vice and promotion of virtue"—whom I'd encountered during a trip to Kabul in 1998. Their behavior was contradictory. They were frightened by the fact that I was menstruating, and would not permit me to take a shower until they were sure that "the blood had finished," but then they insisted I wash all my clothes to clean myself thoroughly. As a uniform, I was assigned pajamas and a bathrobe like those that Arab women wear, underwear (fairly sexy), and a pair of plastic sandals. After that, when I had to wash the clothes I was wearing, I put my "civilian" clothes back on, with a certain pleasure, moreover, because wearing my own clothes gave me the sensation of being back in my own skin. The "Karbalites" seemed obsessed with dirt and uncleanliness: they were always washing their underpants and undershirts and hanging them on full display in the common bathroom. What's more, when I washed my own clothes one of them would come and make sure that I scrubbed the collar of my pajama shirt sufficiently. "You'll become a good person this way," Hussein would tell me. And when I emphasized that I washed my own clothes in Rome as well, and not always in the washing machine, either, he seemed surprised. Once they also made me wash the floor of the bathroom; I don't know if this was intended as a further humiliation, but frankly, I couldn't have cared less: it was a way to kill time and certainly better than sitting in my locked room in the dark. And I took the occasion to show them how one really washes a floor, as opposed to how they did it, even though they were always disinfecting everything. In this kind of behavior—jokingly squirting me with water, for instance—I did not detect the rigorous Islamic attitude of men who won't even shake a woman's hand, because she is impure. Abbas sometimes told me that I was dirty because I wasn't Muslim. From the tone it was hard to tell if he believed it, or if it was only a joke. Certainly the rush to shake my hand when they announced my release—"Congratulations, you're off to Rome"—had little to do with a confirmed Wahhabist's rules of behavior. In some ways this saved me, because if my abductors had been Islamic fundamentalists they would not have ignored my political commitment and beliefs. My book, *The Slavery of the Veil,* my militancy against Islamic integralism, standing alongside Muslim women (Algerian, Afghani, etc.) in the fight for their rights, would all have been used against me. And in fact—this, too, I would only find out later—some of my articles on these issues had been translated into Arabic and distributed on a fundamentalist Web site. Perhaps in an excess of zeal, someone had attributed to me a book by a young Russian journalist on female suicide bombers in Chechnya, called *The Betrothed of Allah*—a book I had only reviewed. For those working for my freedom, from comrades at *Il Manifesto* to women who shared my opposition to fundamentalism, one of the biggest concerns was to avoid emphasizing this part of my work, a difficult task in the Internet age. In any case, friends and Arab journalists—particularly the associations of Algerian women—were very careful when speaking publicly about this, as they were well aware of the risks I faced.

Luckily, this was one risk I avoided. My kidnappers were not Salafists, despite their show of religious devotion—due perhaps more to the fact that in Iraq, Islam is fast becoming the unifying element in the fight against the occupation and the West.

RE-ISLAMIZATION

When nationalism fails, one turns to religion as an element of identity; in this, other Arab countries, such as Algeria, have preceded Iraq. The process of "Islamizing" a secular country—and Iraq was a secular country under the Baath Party, which was vaguely socialist-inspired—had already begun after the first Gulf War. Even the "conversion" of Saddam Hussein in 1991 was probably more a bid to criminals, who were tried and punished according to the dictates of shari'a. The next step would be the hunt for representatives of the past regime. At the same time, the Hawza prevented military forces from entering the sacred cities, which thus remained under the control of the religious authorities. One notable exception was when U.S. troops penetrated to the heart of Najaf in pursuit of the followers of Muqtada al Sadr, after a warrant had been issued against him for the killing of Abd al Khoi (son of the famous Ayatollah Abdul Qasem, stabbed to death in a mosque on April 10, 2003, shortly after his return from exile). During the crisis, the American mortars did not respect even the most sacred places, including the mausoleum of the Imam Ali and the great cemetery of the city, where many Shiites ask to be buried in order to be near the founder of the sect. The bloody clashes ended only with the mediation of al Sistani, who thus again took control of the city. And with the elections of 2005, this control reached all the way to the government, when al Sistani sponsored a sectarian slate of candidates (even issuing a fatwa in their upport) that proved victorious. The results are clearly visible. By w, the only challenger to the major Shiite religious leader is Muq- a al Sadr, who owes his popularity to the fame of his father, Mo- med Sadeq, assassinated in Najaf in 1999. The younger, more s Muqtada set up his strongholds in Kufa, near Najaf, and in ity, the enormous Shiite quarter in Baghdad once called Sad- y, now renamed after the venerated ayatollah. But not even , who harangues the crowds with his fiery discourses, can ding to the will of al Sistani at least some of the time, as in s of January 30, 2005. He himself did not vote, but he did lowers to vote, and placed his own candidates on several s—thus, many of his followers, including representa- l Mahdi, the militia that has often been involved in vith the American occupiers, went to the polls.

guarantee support from the Arab masses than a demonstration of newfound faith. And in fact, it was only after 1991 that one began to hear the calls of the muezzin in Iraqi streets, to see the official observance of Ramadan, to note that alcohol was now sold only in special stores and could not be consumed in public, not even in hotels mostly frequented by foreigners. It was a showy Islamization, almost vulgar, like that of the Um al Marik Mosque (later rebaptized al Qura), which represents, as its name indicates, the "mother of all battles" and bears minarets in the shape of scud missiles and Kalashnikovs and a lake around its base in the shape of the Arab nations. Next door is a sort of tabernacle, which hosts a copy of the Koran, written, they say, in the blood of Saddam. I attempted to see it many times, but was never successful—each time I tried, the guards were out, or they were doing maintenance work. Baghdad was full of monumental mosques under construction when the war began. One of these, built on terrain recovered from an ex-airport, was supposed to be the biggest in the world, reflecting Saddam Hussein's mania for size, and would have borne his name, like almost all the monumental constructions in Iraq. No one dared take down the towering cranes used in its construction, though they were a slap in the face for the millions of Iraqis suffering the disastrous effects of the embargo.

This display of religious symbolism mirrors the crusade of George W. Bush, which claims to make war in order to "export democracy" but in reality results in the imposition of a theocratic regime. The power vacuum created by the violent overthrow of the dictator has in fact simply been filled by the only forces who were able—through a network of mosques—to preserve some form of organization through the dark and bloody days of Saddam's reign. The mosques were not, thus, only places of prayer and recruitment, but also of fund raising: Sunni mosques were supported by Saddam, while those of the holy Shiite cities enjoy even now notable revenue from the constant stream of pilgrims, both Iraqi and foreign. It must be added that a recognized clerical hierarchy also contributes to the reinforcement of Shiite power, whose most important representatives are joined in the Hawza, a sort of Shiite Vatican. The current leader is the authoritative Grand Ayatollah Ali al Sistani, who exercises his power in political circles as well—a choice which may eventually undermine his religious authority. The fatwa handed down by the ayatollah at the beginning of the invasion, in which he instructed Iraqis not to fight the Americans, was received so unfavorably that he was forced to take it back.

Aside from this incident, the Hawza was in control from the very day after the fall of Saddam, unleashing its own mullahs everywhere to guarantee territorial control, even before the representatives of the major Shiite religious parties (the Supreme Council for the Islamic Revolution in Iraq [SCIRI] and the Dawa) had returned from exile.

On April 9, 2003, the Americans had yet to occupy Baghdad—the tanks coming from Najaf were stopped by the Tigris, awaiting the force moving in from Kut—but both the military and government functionaries of the ex-regime had already vanished and the city had fallen prey to looters. These bands continued to act undisturbed while the tanks took possession of the capital. This wasn't an assault on the bread ovens of a hungry populace, but a vendetta that led to the further humiliation of the Iraqi people—at least those who chose to stay clear of the looters and defend their own dignity.

The first to get out in the streets and restore order, right after the arrival of the Americans, were the aforementioned mullahs. Near Saddam City, soon to be renamed Sadr City, I saw armed men stop-

ping suspicious vehicles by firing into the air at a traffic light in front of a mosque. They would search the vehicle, recover the loot, car included, deposit it all in the storerooms of the mosque and arrest those responsible for the most serious thefts. To me, they immediately seemed like a kind of religious police. The confirmation came shortly after, when I met their leader, who turned out to be a mullah sent by the Hawza. The looting that had devastated ministries, warehouses, police stations, and various offices, had not even spared the hospitals, where medical equipment and even old incubators and beds were hauled away.

When I arrived at al Kindi, one of the city's major hospitals, th situation was desperate. Now that there was nothing more to an American tank had appeared on the street corner. The m staff, who had also been treating civilian victims of the asked in vain for help from the marines. The sick had bee return home—at least those who could make it. The o' yond help. Finally, the doctors turned to the relig The hospital was now in the hands of two mull one Shiite, who were trying to restore the sto back personnel. To guarantee security, th would later become the religious militia. feet and imposed Islamic rigor over i that one day an acquaintance of mi her father, was almost unable to o' not wearing the veil. Only her on duty to admit the old m mosques that compensa thanks to the medicine

It began like this, and of religious order.

The other face of this religious influence is the imposition of shari'a in the Shiite south, in a version closer to the Iranian model. The Iranian influence is very strong, not only because al Sistani is Iranian, but because the Shiite religious parties—the Supreme Council for the Islamic Revolution and the Dawa—are pro-Iranian, stemming from their years in exile in Tehran during the regime of Saddam. Muqtada al Sadr, who has remained in Iraq, also has religious ties in Iran, in Qom. His seat in Karbala, like those of the other Shiite religious parties, is always full of Iranian "counselors." By now, the *pasdaran* (Iranian nongovernmental militia) are at home in Iraq, even though al Sistani is not a supporter of the theories of Ayatollah Khomeini, which call for *al velayat e faqih* (supremacy of religion). Sistani does not want power to be directly wielded by the mullahs. Al Sistani's line of thinking does not signify a refusal of political participation, but rather the safeguarding of the religious: religion may contaminate politics, but not vice versa. Despite his strong influence over the constitution passed in August of 2005, Sistani was not able to impose an Islamic state, nor shari'a as the only law, even though Islam represents the new identity of Iraq and has become the religion of the state. The doors are now open to the possibility, however: all it requires is patience, and the elderly leader (who was born in Mashhad in 1930 and studied in Qom before moving to Najaf) has already demonstrated that he has plenty. Most importantly, whatever he has so far been unable to obtain in the Green Zone—from the Iraqi government and its American protectors—he has already won on the ground.

The religious influence has gotten stronger in the Sunni camp as well, even though the more loosely organized Sunnis don't recognize a clerical hierarchy; therefore, there is no one representative personality like al Sistani. Still, Islam has become the bond that ties together the heterogeneous forces opposing the Bush crusade. And the Council of the Ulema, which gathers together the most representative Sunni religious figures, becomes the point of reference to pass on political instructions—particularly through the sermons delivered during Friday prayers—to mediate conflicts and to condemn any deviation from the resistance.

If the conservative Shiites are inspired by the Iranian model, the Sunni fundamentalists look to the Wahhabist school of the Saudis, which has for several years sent its own emissaries to Iraq in order to proselytize in observant Sunni areas such as Mosul and Falluja. It's a sort of re-Islamization that finds traction in the most conservative sectors still under tribal control. Tribal power and religious conservatism feed a part of the resistance in areas like Falluja, without reaching the extremes of jihad propagated by Al Qaeda terrorists. In the mosques, the resistance has a ready-made gathering place where it can spread propaganda. Nevertheless, Wahhabist extremism, instead of uniting, divides the resistance and in some cases scares off the population with its harsh rules and whipping of young people who drink beer or listen to music. The worst fate, of course, falls to the women, in both the Sunni and the Shiite camps. Religious order and the specter of an Islamic republic scare laypeople and Christians, and many of these have already abandoned the country. Women who do not wear the Islamic veil are threatened and often stop going out of the house for fear of a disfiguring attack with acid. Christian children are afraid for their safety at school. Even the churches have seen a decline in their congregations after the attacks they have suffered.

In the two weeks following the major terrorist attacks against churches in August of 2004, almost 40,000 Christians—out of a total of 750,000 (3 percent of the population), a majority of them Chaldeans (Eastern Catholics without ties to Rome but who respect the Pope)—abandoned Iraq, according to the figures of then minister of immigration, Pascale Warda. The major part of these fleeing Christians took refuge in Syria and Jordan, waiting for better times, but those who could left to join relatives in Australia or in Sweden, where there have been established Iraqi communities for some time. Persecution of Christians in Mesopotamia is nothing new, but Saddam's bloody regime had been tolerant of Christians, guaranteeing the right of worship, although not that of proselytizing.

Today the charge of Christian proselytizing is often associated with that of spying for the Americans. It's a charge that is often not unfounded: many American sects have moved into Iraq under the cover of NGOs—they have plenty of money, and in return for conversion they promise aid and above all the false prospect of a visa for the United States.

Another of the many Iraqi paradoxes: one of the most secular of the Arab states has now fallen into the hands of the religious parties and militias.

SEVEN

WOMEN

I HAVE always felt ill at ease when I'm forced to live exclusively with men. And yet I've often been in that situation, traveling in Arab, Muslim countries: bars filled with men; streets invaded by young guys leaning on the walls (*hittistes*), like in the dark years of Algeria; men on the streets of Kabul followed by ghostlike women, hidden under their burkas; buses with separate entrances for men and women, like they have in Iran. Mutilated societies. Until recently, Iraq was not one of them, but it risks becoming one now: actually, it's already in the process of transformation.

When I found myself locked in my room/cell, watched over by two male guards, my mind wandered back to Kabul, in May of 1998, during the years of the Taliban. At that time I happened to be the only guest and the only woman in the Hotel Intercontinental. Few signs remained of the hotel's former splendor, and ongoing armed clashes between "theology students," who controlled the capital, and the Tajik mujahideen, who were attacking from the north, had blasted huge rents in the walls. At night, I was truly terrified: I would hear male voices chasing through the dark corridors, doors slamming, the ring of some far-off bell, just like in a horror film. After having piled the sparse furnishings in front of the door, there was nothing to do but stare out the hotel window at the few faint lights in the distance. I would wait for the sunrise, hoping that nothing would happen, because there was no one to come to my aid. Telephones didn't work and the transceiver lent me by an official with the World Food Program was practically useless, since I didn't know how it worked. I was frightened and lonely, but what I missed the most, I realized, was the companionship of women. There were no women to be found: the Taliban had forbidden women to work, and they certainly couldn't frequent hotels reserved for foreigners. For men, it was a different story: in fact the Taliban often held their meetings at the hotel, eating in the restaurant, while I was forced to eat hidden behind a screen.

Iraq is not Afghanistan under the Taliban—but for me, it was still a prison. Yet there was a difference between the terror of Kabul and that of Baghdad: although I was a prisoner here, and thus entirely in my abductors' power, I never feared sexual violence. In truth, I never suffered any physical violence; I was never even bound or blindfolded, except at the moment of my release. Still, I thought the presence of a woman would be reassuring for me. But that was precisely what my abductors didn't want: to reassure me. They were forced to allow me some female contact a few days after my abduction, however, when I pounded violently on the door, yelling: "I'm not well. Call a woman: I have 'female trouble.'" And so, after a bit, a woman came to find out what I needed, later sending clothes and some medicine, along with shampoo, a comb, a toothbrush (although I had to wait weeks for some toothpaste) and even a moisturizing cream, since my skin was growing dry and scaly from sitting in the dark. A woman came: I heard her, I spoke to her, but I never saw her, since she was entirely veiled. "Call me whatever you want," she said. "Karima?" Maybe. She wouldn't even grant me the certainty of a false name, and it was hard to invent one for such a ghostly figure—even her hands were hidden from view, covered by long gloves. She guessed at my discomfort as a woman surrounded exclusively by men; she alluded to it, but she showed me no tenderness. Perhaps this was simply her down-to-earth female demeanor, or stemmed from her own situation as a woman, a condition of which I knew nothing. Yet under that black cloth I could sense a woman who was strong, willful, educated—she spoke Arabic, English, and French all correctly—and very shrewd. Could this possibly be her daily dress? I couldn't believe it, although she wore the veil with a certain confidence and elegance, almost as though she were used to it. But she wasn't as submissive as her dress would have you believe, I would almost swear to it.

I tried asking for her help at other times, despite her harshness, but her presence was rarely granted. It seemed that when I asked about her, my guards would get scared, as though they feared her. Or maybe they feared something else that I couldn't understand? It was as though they believed women were dangerous; perhaps they feared me as well. Sometimes I would delude myself on that point, particularly when they seemed happy at the idea that the moment of my liberation was approaching, or when Abbas would order me to cry: "Why don't you cry?" Actually, I marveled at that myself: usually I cry over everything, and yet as a captive, tears came to my eyes only once. It was during the filming of the first video, when my abductors told me to appeal to my companion: they were tears of rage, mostly, and of emotion. I was overloading Pier with the weight of freeing me, as though everything depended on him. I didn't want to do it, but I had no choice. And if they didn't free me after all? It was the first time—and I feared it might be the last—that I had addressed him since the cursed fourth of February. Before that, we spoke every day, sharing the results of my work, my successes and failures, my daily problems and fears. Now I felt tremendously alone. And then, my eyes would fill with tears when I spoke of my family. I had a terrible sense of guilt about my parents. They're elderly, how could they bear all this? And since I didn't give him the satisfaction of seeing me cry, Abbas would tell me: "Think of your family." Was this pure sadism? Why did he want to exult in my weakness? He didn't succeed in his efforts, in any event, and since I remained resolutely dry-eyed, he concluded: "Crying would be a relief, you would sleep better afterward." He might even have been right, but I didn't cry then, or ever. Until my return. Now I've started crying again, excessively— maybe I'm weeping all the tears I stored up during those weeks.

The woman, instead, was straightforward, to the point of cruelty. When one of my kidnappers told me: "I give you my word, we won't kill you," she had added: "they haven't decided yet, but if he gave you his word…." But then she asked my favorite color, in order to buy the clothes I would wear during captivity, as though color could alleviate the nightmare. My favorite color is green, but in that context I would never have said so, and in that moment I preferred black anyway. It was more appropriate. I wasn't able to have the kind of exchange I wished for with that invisible woman, who appeared only in moments of emergency. It just wasn't possible. But I was curious about a woman so evidently strong, cloaked in a garment of total submission. And at the moment of my release, when I asked for similar clothes to camouflage me in case the Americans stopped us on the street, they said no. I had to be who I was. Only they could dissimulate or disguise themselves, so as not to be recognized.

In some ways, that woman represented a challenge for me. I could sense her dignity, which even those cumbersome garments couldn't hide, and that spurred me to defend my own dignity successfully. Despite the veils that erased the shape of her body, she inspired me to care for my own body. "Move around, otherwise you won't even be able to walk when it's time to go." And so I began to exercise. "You've lost so much weight, you're too thin," she said. I had no mirrors; I sensed my weight loss only when I put my jeans back on to wash my pajamas, or when I slid them on in secret, just for the sake of feeling back in my own clothes, to recapture a little of my former self.

In trying to decipher that woman I thought of all the women I'd met during my past travels: the Algerians who risked their lives rather than submit to Islamic dictates; the Afghans, who under the Taliban and the mujahideen had so internalized the conviction that their security was guaranteed by the burka that they could no longer free themselves from it. I thought above all of the many Iraqi women I'd met during my numerous trips to their country. I thought of Fawzia, who had been persecuted for much of her life because she was a communist, but who had never left Iraq, even though she and her husband spent years in prison. I thought of Khalifa Zakya, a stage actress who had been imprisoned, her life only spared by Saddam because of her broad popularity, and who now does humanitarian work with women and orphans. I thought of Um Nidal, an activist with the historic League of Iraqi Women, the country's first women's organization, founded in the 1950s during the monarchy. I always found her, with her head of beautiful white hair, working in the League's "new" offices (actually the wreck of an ex-military recruitment center). The League had been recently revived by activists who had returned from abroad, or from Kurdistan, where many—including Nidal herself—had taken refuge from Saddam. I thought of Mithal, with her large green eyes, who had been tortured and imprisoned at Abu Ghraib for eighty days, and whom I'd seen again just two days before my abduction. She was the only ex-inmate of the infamous prison to speak of her experiences: having been through an American prison and suffered sexual assault made her indelibly guilty in the eyes of her society; these women are marked for life, as are their daughters. Upon release from Abu Ghraib some women have killed themselves, while others have been murdered. It's difficult to gather precise data on this phenomenon, because no one wants to talk about it. The subject is taboo. I thought of Yanar Mohammed as well, a secular woman, president of the Organization for the Freedom of Women in Iraq, who had received death threats from Islamist groups.

CRIMES OF HONOR

Since the beginning of the occupation there has been a steady rise in cases of domestic violence, and particularly in the number of "crimes of honor," already common under Saddam, according to the legal office of the Baghdad morgue. "Killed in order to cleanse her disgrace," state many of the autopsy certificates compiled by Faeq Ameen Bakr, general director of Baghdad's Institute of Forensic Medicine. These are cases in which the women are killed by their own families to avenge their honor—on the instructions of religious or tribal leaders, who now substitute for an organized system of justice. "The numbers have risen after the fall of Saddam," says Doctor Bakr, although he adds, "it's difficult to verify the number because often these crimes are hidden." The motives are varied: a woman refuses to marry the man chosen by her family, or she marries someone her parents don't approve of and gets pregnant, or she is raped (four hundred women were raped in the first four months of the occupation, according to the Organization for the Freedom of Women in Iraq). In any case, crimes of honor go practically unpunished: the culprit is pursued by the law only if he turns himself in, and even in these cases, sentences are a maximum of three years, with most getting less than six months.

And it's not only crimes of honor that women are dealing with. Rabiah, a forty-year-old woman, is afraid to go out of the house. When she was younger, she worked for a government ministry, but since her salary was too low to cover the cost of a babysitter for her two children, she eventually quit her job. Once her children were grown, she went back to college to get a diploma as an interpreter— she wanted to change careers. Then the war began. In contrast to the rest of her family, she did not flee the country, believing her place was in Iraq. Now the disaster provoked by the occupation has her seriously worried. She refuses to wear the veil, as the Islamists would like, and she is particularly terrified by the fact that justice is now in the hands of tribal and religious leaders. Rabiah no longer leaves the house alone—she has her husband or one of her sons accompany her—because if she got in a car accident, according to a tribal custom once again in use, the injured party could demand a woman in payment, to use according to his pleasure. How long will this go on? "It will take decades. And to think that before the war we would say 'go ahead and start so we can get it over with,'" said a resigned Rabiah, when I met her in a residential quarter of Baghdad.

The climate has also worsened in universities: campuses have ended up under the control of Islamist organizations that claim the right to separate the sexes in various departments, and use threats and physical violence to control student behavior and dress (girls can no longer wear pants and use of the veil is obligatory). The result? Every day there are fewer women on the streets of Baghdad. And they are not only less numerous, but less visible: they sidle away in their long skirts, almost uniformly veiled, as though they hope no one will notice them. To hear them come to life, to speak, you have to go to the market or to a big department store, where you can lose yourself among them in front of a display of cosmetics and find a feminine bond, or crowd around a fruit stand where everyone is complaining about prices that seem always higher. More and more husbands are starting to replace them even on these daily errands. It's not a lightening of their load, however: often, doing the shopping represents the only pretext for getting out of the house. But some women have disappeared while going to the market. Jobs are nonexistent; even the women who had jobs have lost them, and the withdrawal of many NGOs has penalized them further. The war and the occupation have provoked a cultural regression that the Islamist movement feeds, imposing its own religious precepts: women should stay at home and leave the work to men, given that there's so little of it, and if they insist on going out, they must be veiled. "Women have two choices: face the threat of rape and subsequent murder at the hands of their families, or seclusion at home," says Amal al Mualimchi, a women's rights activist.

The security for women that everyone calls for in Iraq means protection against the violence of the occupation, against terrorism, abuses of power, kidnapping, and rape. But how can you protect the women who are beaten, tortured, and raped in their own homes every day? OFWI, the Organization for the Freedom of Women in Iraq—founded in 1993 in Sulaimaniya (Kurdistan)—extended its activities throughout the country after the fall of Saddam. In the summer of 2004, it founded the first shelter in Baghdad for abused women or those at risk for being killed in "crimes of honor." The location of the shelter is secret. It consists of just two rooms and a kitchen, where currently, "eight women are living," as Hadil Jawad told me when I met her on the eve of my abduction in the offices of the organization. It's a small building with a garden, right in the city center, monitored by armed guards. Hadil greets the young women who come seeking help with an open, reassuring smile. She's not much older than thirty, with a sunny demeanor, and there's nothing to indicate that she, too, has shared their horrible experiences. Yet she was one of the shelter's first guests, when she ended up in Sulaimaniya, escaping a father who wanted to kill her. She had fled Baghdad in 1993 with her sweetheart, but hers was no romantic adventure. "I come from a traditional family that could not tolerate the idea that a woman can choose a husband for love. I was seventeen when I fell in love with a neighbor. Our relationship continued for four years, but my family would not allow me to marry him—also because I am a Sunni and he is Shiite. When my father realized that I had made up my mind to marry him, he began to beat me, to lock me in the house, and he tried to force me to marry a cousin. There was no choice but to flee: we got married and then we ran away to the north, first to Kirkuk and then to Sulaimaniya, because my father threatened to kill me. When he couldn't find me, he also threatened my husband's father." Hadil returned to her own city only when OFWI opened an office in Baghdad. "If you could choose, would you do it again?" I asked her. "Certainly I would. I'm happy, I have a three-year-old daughter, but I'm sorry for my sisters, who had to suffer the consequences: after I ran away, my older sister's husband left her; another was forced to marry an old man, and the youngest had to leave school." Hadil smiles, but every time she goes out the door she's terrified by the idea that someone might recognize her. "But you can't live in seclusion your entire life," she sighs. Her smile hides many secrets—not only hers, but also those of the women who turn to her, thanks to the announcements published in the organization's newspaper, *Al Mousawat* (Equality).

RAPES OF THE OCCUPATION

There are other broken lives, like that of Liqa, a twenty-six-year-old currently hospitalized for mental illness. She cannot speak, but she allows Hadil to tell me of her tragic experience. She wants to make it known, because at grave personal risk, Liqa went looking for justice in the Green Zone, where the U.S. command is located. Yet her search was in vain. Here is her story. In April of 2003, when the Americans occupied Baghdad, Liqa found work in a snack bar on a U.S. base at the airport. Other Iraqi women worked with her, but there was one soldier named Harlow (at least that's what she remembers) who always followed her, particularly when she went to the bathroom. She tried to avoid him, but it was no use. One day, the soldier offered her a drink. "There was nothing wrong with accepting it, and it was awkward to refuse." But the drink had been doctored with a drug. She felt ill, passed out, and when she awoke she discovered she had been raped. There was no doubt that the rapist was Harlow, who was even boasting about it to his fellow soldiers. Desperate and furious, Liqa denounced the assault to a colonel, who promised to take action. She deluded herself into thinking that he would force Harlow to marry her, the only compensation possible in a society like that of Iraq: she was no longer a virgin and now she would not be able to find another husband. But the measure the colonel had in mind was quite different: after a few days, the soldier disappeared, probably sent home, and with his departure went any hope of compensation. When she realized what had happened, she screamed at the colonel and he kicked her off the base. Desperate, without her honor or her job, and unable to return home out of fear that her family would kill her, she turned to Hadil's association. Here they found her an attorney who could help her file a rape charge with the Coalition Provisional Authority, which still existed at the beginning of 2004 (it was dissolved in June of the same year). Liqa gathered her courage and entered the American fortress: she went to the convention center inside the Green Zone, where she had to undergo a gynecological examination. In the end, the doctor declared that she was no longer a virgin but that there were no signs of rape. Her case was handed over to an Iraqi woman, Shakla, who worked with the Americans on cases of reparations for damages provoked by the occupying forces. But one fine day Shakla, too, disappeared, and Liqa fell into a deep depression. Liqa was not the only rape victim—her friend Intisar, who worked with her at the bar, had been raped by the same soldier, but had not had the courage to report it, and continued to work at the base. She met with Liqa a couple of times, but then Liqa heard nothing more.

Only later would I learn, from an article published in the British daily *Guardian* (March 8, 2005), that soldiers from the Third Infantry Brigade, the same unit that fired on the car I was traveling in after I was set free, had been investigated the year before for the rape of Iraqi women. The charges were contained in a twelve hundred–page document that the British daily had obtained from the American Civil Liberties Union. Four soldiers were accused of having raped two Iraqi women while they were on duty at a base snack bar! Many soldiers had been interrogated, but no one interviewed the women. "I just know the women were Iraqi. But I don't know if they were raped, or if they were prostitutes, or just wanted to have sex," one soldier told the investigators. So, in the end, the case was closed for lack of evidence.

Other cases of sexual assault also went unpunished. One such incident involved two young sisters, aged fourteen and fifteen. They were from a very poor family, and had been hanging around the American soldiers camped out in the ex-Baath Party headquarters in Sowera, an agricultural center on the Tigris, around seventy kilometers south of Baghdad. One night, at the beginning of July 2003, the two girls were raped and beaten almost to death. Dumped in front of a nearby hospital, one subsequently died while the other disappeared. According to murmurs I heard from acquaintances in the village—where open discussion of the news, which had leaked out through hospital workers, was taboo—the surviving girl had been assassinated by relatives, at the urging of tribal and religious leaders.

Women are thus victims of the Americans, of a conservative society, and of Islamist fanatics, who, after the fall of Saddam, are the ones dictating the laws. Sometimes the victims are very young.

Rana is wandering around the back of the OFWI offices. She's the youngest guest among the women who have taken shelter here, and has been entrusted to a family so she can continue her studies. She's sixteen years old, full of life, but with a lot of suffering behind her, which she tries unsuccessfully to conceal beneath her modern dress: jeans, a T-shirt, and a cap with a visor just large enough to hide a few touches of makeup. She comes from southern Iraq, where the society is even more traditional and conservative. Her weak-willed parents were completely subservient to their sons, and cared nothing for their daughters. One sister even died after a beating from her brothers resulted in brain damage. Rana was not permitted to go to school. "I couldn't stand it anymore," she says. "My brothers beat me all the time, so I decided to run away from home. I hitched a ride, but the driver wanted to abduct me, so I opened the door and threw myself out. I was hurt, so I was taken to an American base nearby. I stayed there for two months. Then the Americans said I couldn't stay any more. Iraqi law didn't allow it. One day a cleric came to see me, evidently sent by my brother. He forced me to go back home. According to my uncle, my brothers should have killed me for what I had done. I was miserable. I never spoke anymore, I just wanted to kill myself. To 'cure' me, a cleric burned me on my head and body." And she showed me her scars. "This went on until one day I managed to run away again and make it to Baghdad. I had saved the address of OFWI—I found it in the magazine *Al Mousawat.*" Rana says that her brothers belong to an Islamist group founded by the Iranians that has been proselytizing in the south. But she won't add anything further, out of fear. Her facade of youthful defiance doesn't quite hide her insecurity as she faces a future full of unknowns.

SHARI'A IS ALREADY LAW

The Islamization of Iraq and of political life—under way even before the victory of the Shiite slate sponsored by Ayatollah al Sistani in the January 2005 elections, and reinforced by the priority assigned to Islam as an indispensable pillar of the Iraqi constitution—raises fears of a drastic reduction of women's rights. Although he introduced some limitations in later years, such as requiring women under forty-five to travel abroad only with an escort, Saddam Hussein had continued to enforce the 1959 family code, considered one of the most progressive in the Arab-Muslim world. On December 29, 2003, however, SCIRI leader Ayatollah Abdelaziz al Hakim took advantage of his turn as president of the governing council to launch "Measure 137," which abolished the family code still in force and replaced it with shari'a, the law of the Koran. Only an immediate mobilization of women, including some government ministers, uncovered and blocked the Shiite leader's maneuver. The contradiction Iraqis now face is that the Americans, who had supported the presence of women in parliament (with a 25 percent quota), are ready to compromise on Islamic law, opening the door to a theocracy. And in this case, women are once again the primary victims. Conscious of the dangers they faced, various women's organizations set their sights on the referendum of October 15, 2005, launching a campaign against the constitution with the slogan "Our Vote for Our Rights." Their efforts were to no avail—the constitution was ratified. In the January 2005 elections, I had spoken to Shiite and Christian women at the polls who were voting for the hated ex-premier Iyad Allawi—considered a CIA puppet—just because he was a strong, and above all secular, figure, in order to oppose the feared Islamist onslaught (which proved victorious anyway, in all but the Kurdish zones).

The country is already feeling the effects. Shari'a is by now reality in Basra, for example, a city of a million and a half residents in southern Iraq, where followers of the radical Shiite leader Muqtada al Sadr have imposed their will. On March 28, 2005, during a picnic in a Basra park, around four hundred engineering students were attacked by a group of thirty Islamists armed with clubs, knives, and Kalashnikovs. They fell on the students, accusing them of being "infidels," but they were particularly incensed with the girls, calling them prostitutes. "I was sitting with some friends at the edge of the garden, when a masked man, dressed in black, came up to us and asked, in a threatening way, why we weren't wearing the *hijab* [the Islamic veil]. I felt a blow to my head. There was panic everywhere, I heard kids yelling, and shots fired in the air. While I was trying to find a way out, I was hit a second time, with an iron bar. I blacked out for a few minutes," recounted Celia Garabet, a twenty-one-year-old Christian girl, to Delphine Minoui (*Le Figaro*, April 11, 2005). Since then, she no longer leaves the house. Sheikh Assad al Basri, Muqtada's representative in Basra, claims responsibility for the action: "Only with violence can we stop this moral slide, and we're ready to do it again, if necessary.... During the picnic, girls were wearing shirts that were too thin, and boys were dancing. It's immoral!" They have managed to impose the veil on Muslim girls. They prevent male doctors from treating women patients in the maternity wards in city hospitals. In short, they have installed a climate of terror. Juliana Youssef Davud, an English teacher, remembers the splendors of Basra before the arrival of Saddam, before the war with Iran and the first Gulf War, and everything that has followed. "When I was my students' age, we went to the movies. On the weekends, we'd go to the casino on the coast, and then meet up at the cabaret. We drank beer, we'd organize picnics every week. None of these small pleasures is allowed anymore," this elegant teacher sighed to reporter Delphine Minoui. In those days, Davud even wore a miniskirt, just like the women of Kabul, who before the arrival of the Islamists stayed out late in what was then considered one of the region's capitals of entertainment and culture.

We can only hope that Iraq doesn't meet the same end as Afghanistan!

EIGHT

ANOTHER LEBANON

"DOESN'T HE look like Santa Claus?" Abbas was referring to Grand Ayatollah Ali al Sistani, the seventy-five-year-old, white-bearded Shiite leader who by now appears in public only rarely. When they ask me about Iraqi political or religious figures, I always keep my answers vague. It's better not to compromise myself: who knows what my abductors really think? I did the same thing when Abbas showed me his pistol and said: "See, there's a picture of Saddam on it." I hadn't even seen it without my glasses—and I was reluctant to pull them out for fear they'd be taken from me, like all my other personal effects—but given that pictures of Saddam were everywhere, I just nodded. "What do you think of Saddam?" I instantly sensed a trick question. "You're the ones who have to choose who governs you. I'm an Italian—I have to deal with who should govern Italy. I'm against making war to overthrow a government, or subjecting an entire population to a thirteen-year embargo. I can fight against that in my own country, but here, the choice is up to you, not me…." Abbas doesn't pursue the issue, although he returns to it later. He never talks about the Sunni religious leaders, however, or the Council of the Ulema. My guards go from trying to pass themselves off as Shiites—with their choice of battle names—to ridiculing their presumptive leader, Ali al Sistani.

I had already gathered that my abductors were Sunni, and not fundamentalists (or at least, not Wahhabists), despite their show of piety. Yet their rancor against the Shiites sometimes became palpable, particularly when they speak of commemorative rites for Shiite imams, or the recent January 2005 elections, held just a few days before my abduction.

The vertical split between Sunnis and Shiites, not to speak of the Kurds, is evident by now at every level of Iraqi society. And yet, just a few years ago, before the war, that wasn't the case. Families, in most cases, were mixed: marriages between Shiites, Sunnis, and Kurds took place within even the biggest tribes, where one often found Sunnis and Shiites together. I had seen an example at the home of my interpreter, Wael: I was there to interview his father, Salman Dawood al Bayati, who had been the former secretary of Iraqi labor unions before being accused of conspiracy (a method used by Saddam to get rid of anyone who might pose an alternative to his absolute power). The father was Sunni, the mother was Shiite, and Wael, who is Sunni on his father's side, had married a Sunni Kurd. Now, a mixed marriage would be unthinkable: you no longer look outside your own tribe to find a husband or wife, let alone outside your religious community. In fact, when Hussein, my jailer, spoke of his own possible future marriage, he was planning to marry a cousin.

The clashes between Sunnis, Shiites, and Kurds have intensified in the last months, and the U.S. above all has played a large role in encouraging the division of the country. The partition of Iraq, with the aim of controlling it, has been a Western goal since the no-fly zones (patrolled airspace south of the thirty-second parallel and north of the thirty-sixth that was off-limits to Saddam's airplanes) were first established right after the war of 1991. Officially, the zones were supposed to protect the Kurds in the north and the Shiites in the south, but this did not prevent them both from being massacred by Saddam's army after their attempted insurrection was first encouraged (and then abandoned) by Washington. The no-fly zones were thus a precursor of a country divided in three: Kurds in the north, Sunnis in the center, and Shiites in the south. The occupation has followed a similar design, gaining leverage from the old rancor against Saddam, who had repressed Kurds and Shiites, and against the Sunnis in general, who, despite being a minority (around 20 percent of the 25 million Iraqis) have governed the country without interruption since independence in 1932, at the time of the monarchy.

The aim of partition is furthered by the assignment of contracts for rebuilding. The first sections of infrastructure to be partially restored were telecommunications centers (which had also been the first to be destroyed at the beginning of the bombing). There had been no mobile phone network under Saddam; one was now created by dividing the country in three. The north was assigned to a Turkish/Iraqi company, the center to an Egyptian/Iraqi company, and the south to a Kuwaiti/Iraqi company. Most importantly, the three networks are not connected to each other: from Baghdad, you can call Italy on a cell phone but not Basra or Sulaimaniya. This is nothing new: in the Balkans, one of the first signs of the future partition of Yugoslavia was the partition of the phone lines.

Moreover, the Iraqis had divided themselves by their differing reactions to the American intervention. The Kurds had always supported the American army. The Shiites had a more ambiguous attitude: they took advantage of the coalition intervention to liberate themselves from Saddam's repression, maintaining (whether they believed it or not) that once the dictator was gone the Americans would leave as well. Among the Shiites, however, the radical leader Muqtada al Sadr had always declared himself against the occupiers, confronting them with his Jaish al Mahdi, the Mahdi militia (from the name of the late twelfth imam, whose return they await) in heavy fighting in Najaf and Sadr City. The Sunnis, favored by Saddam and the historic holders of power in Iraq, have been the most ferocious opponents of the occupation: they have lost their power and with it, their dignity. It is they who feed the ranks of the resistance and in some cases the terrorism of al Zarqawi. Al Zarqawi dreams of the confrontation between Sunnis and apostate Shiites. In fact, if you believe the revelations made in the *New York Times* on February 9, 2004, on the discovery of a letter sent via CD from the leader of the terrorist organization al Tawheed to Osama bin Laden, the strategy proposed by al Zarqawi is to fight "the greatest cowards created by God." The reference is to the Shiites. The letter reads: "The solution, God alone knows, is to drag the Shiites into battle. It is the only way to prolong the duration of our battle against the infidels. If we succeed in dragging them into a sectarian war, the Sunnis will awaken because they fear destruction and death at the hands of the Shiites." Whether or not al Zarqawi's group is behind the subsequent attacks on Shiite mosques, the victims among the Shiite faithful since then have been in the hundreds. On a Web site, al Zarqawi has celebrated the death of Shiites, disdainfully calling them "monkeys," and characterizing their religion as an "affront to God." At the beginning, the Grand Ayatollah Ali al Sistani had tried to avoid reprisals by inviting Shiites to concentrate on the electoral process. After the elections, however, he asked the new government to "defend the country against mass annihilation." Any solidarity among an occupied people, and particularly among those rebelling against the occupation and thus hardest hit, has crumbled away faster than even al Zarqawi intended—although not, with the exception of some extreme fringe groups, in favor of Al Qaeda.

The opposition between Sunnis and Shiites has only deepened with the worsening national situation, leading to the carnage of August 31, 2005, when almost a thousand people were killed and hundreds wounded among the faithful gathered at the Kadhimiya Mosque to commemorate the seventh imam, Musa al Khadim (Khadim was poisoned in Baghdad in 799 AD on the orders of his rival, Caliph Harun al Rashid). The rumor of a suicide bomber and possibly a small explosion were enough to provoke a panicked stampede, with tragic consequences. The tragedy has assumed a powerful symbolic meaning: a majority of deaths were due to the collapse of the barriers on the bridge that links the Shiite neighborhood of Kadhimiya to that of Adhamiya, on the opposite bank of the Tigris, a stronghold of Sunni resistance. Furthermore, the body of the celebrated "martyr" was thrown into the river from the exact bridge where many of the faithful were killed, before being buried in the monumental Kadhimiya Mosque, which subsequently took his name. After this tragedy, it was as though the division between the religious communities grew even deeper, despite the many gestures of solidarity from the Sunni community to the wounded Shiites. Just a year earlier, during the siege of Najaf in August of 2004, when U.S. troops surrounded the Shiite followers of Muqtada al Sadr, Sunnis had hastened to send help. It was the same in Falluja, under siege in April of 2004, when Shiites and Sunnis organized aid convoys together. But the murder of six Shiite truck drivers in Falluja on June 5 of that year, killed as they were bringing supplies from Sadr City to an American base, gave rise to great indignation. The chilling images of their mutilated bodies were on the front page of several newspapers. The Shiite reprisals were immediate: three Falluja Sunnis were killed in Sadr City. By November of 2004, during the successive and most ferocious attack on Falluja, both Kurds and Shiites were part of the attacking troops, guided by the Americans, though there is no way to know how much of a role they played in the actual fighting.

The creation of security forces and an army represented a new step in the ethnic/sectarian division. The dissolution of Saddam's army had effectively excluded the Sunnis, to whom the ex-dictator had always given favorable career treatment, although he had promoted some Shiite officials during the war against Iran (1980–1988). This was no coincidence: fighting against their Shiite brothers in Iran was intended as a test. At the time, nationalist spirit had prevailed over religious affiliation—Iraqi Shiites are Arabs and not Persians. In fact, the first major defeat inflicted upon the Iranians had been in 1982, at the hands of a Shiite commander. The dictator had in turn exploited the historic opposition of Arabs and Persians for propaganda purposes, setting himself up as a new Saladin and defining the conflict as a "Qadisiyah" of modern times (Qadisiyah was the battle in 637 AD in which the Arabs defeated the Persians, allowing the eastward expansion of Islam). In the wake of this mobilization, at the end of the 1980s, the illusion of a greater integration of Shiites into the country's institutions was born—yet it was an idea that never really materialized. Sunnis remained the privileged elite of the regime, while the Shiites developed culturally (many Shiite intellectuals swelled the ranks of the Communist Party) and expanded economically in the areas where they were a majority, including the capital. The brutally repressed Shiite opposition—like the Kurdish opposition—had been fighting against the regime and Saddam's army since the first Gulf War. Yet only with the recent war and perverse effects of the occupation, which have eased the way for terrorism onto the Iraqi scene, have the differences taken on a strict sectarian and ethnic character.

The elections of January 30, 2005—urged, above all, by the occupiers in order to respect the transition plan and demonstrate the success of the "process of democratization"—were a new step into the abyss of partition. Elections can only be an expression of democracy if—and only if—they represent the crowning result of a process of democratization and popular involvement, not the point of departure for such a process. This is particularly true in a country that is largely spinning out of control and where the fabric of democracy has been shredded, first by the dictatorship, and then by war and occupation. Instead of facilitating the electoral process, the attacks on rebel cities—Samarra, Falluja, Baquba, Ramadi, Mosul—to "cleanse them of insurgents" on the eve of the vote, had the opposite effect: the use of violence demonstrated that freedom of political expression is not possible under occupation, much less freedom to vote. The attacks thus fueled the arguments of those who wanted to stop people from voting. The result? The Sunni community didn't vote— by choice (to protest the occupation); by circumstance (how could the Fallujan refugees vote?); or by force (bowing to threats by armed resistance groups, who vowed to punish the few Sunni voters). An important minority (20 percent) was thus substantially excluded from the process, with the exception of the ex-president Ghazi al Yawar's slate, which elected five deputies to the assembly, out of a total of 275, and aside from a few co-opted members included in the government or involved in the creation of a constitution. The other two communities, the Shiites and the Kurds, did participate in the vote, basically supporting the Bush plan—although it must be remembered that the sectarian Shiite list (United Iraqi Alliance, sponsored by al Sistani, which took 48.2 percent of the vote and 140 seats) included the withdrawal of occupying forces in its party platform.

The images transmitted on Western screens showed only those who voted, without taking into account the reasons of those who did not participate.

This depiction of events reminded me of the famous toppling of the statue of Saddam in Firdaus Square, right after the arrival of the Americans (April 9, 2003). Judging by the images broadcast on Western television, the square seemed to be crowded with exultant Iraqis. In reality, the people of Baghdad were still shut in their houses and the only Iraqis in the square were the assistants of the hundreds of journalists intent on capturing the event.

Election day felt to me like a rerun of the same film, in which you could tell from the first few frames that the movie would end badly. Baghdad was under curfew, and the climate that day was one of imminent catastrophe—much like the feeling on the eve of the American invasion—and not of a holiday celebrating the first free elections after Saddam.

Certainly, Baghdad is not Iraq. In Kurdistan they voted in droves—some people even voted twice—guaranteeing victory to the two established Kurdish parties. The Democratic Party and the Patriotic Union of Kurdistan together took 98 percent of the vote in Kurdistan, and 25.7 percent of the national total. The huge majority of Kurds want independence, as demonstrated by the results of the referendum held alongside the elections. Given the choice between autonomy and independence, 98 percent of the two million participants voted for the latter.

Did Kurdish leaders want this show of strength to give them a boost in their negotiations with Baghdad? Perhaps. But the progressive detachment from Baghdad, which has deepened over the years, sends other signals. There was no Iraqi flag in evidence at the inauguration of the National Assembly of Kurdistan (the regional parliament obtained by the Kurds after 1991) on June 4, 2005, in Erbil, despite the participation of the Iraqi president, the Kurdish Jalal Talabani. What's more, the members of parliament had to swear their loyalty to the unity of the Kurdish region *of Iraq*—yet often they forgot the words "of Iraq." The situation in Kurdistan is very different from the rest of the country: since it supported the American invasion, it suffered little damage in the war, and the region was able to profit from investments that have accelerated its development. In addition, apart from a few extremely bloody cases, Kurdistan has been substantially spared from terrorist attacks, even though the group Ansar al Islam, the only Iraqi group definitively tied to Al Qaeda, had settled in the Kurdish zone of Halabja in 2001. In any event, the Kurdish battle for independence is being fought, for now, in Baghdad: the details of the federalist formula, given the powers attributed to Kurdistan, seem to prefigure a federalist state.

But the crux of the Kurdish question is the allocation of Kirkuk, without which an independent Kurdistan would have no possibility of survival. The city has always been a center of contention: for the Kurds it is Kurdish; in fact, it would be the capital of an independent Kurdistan (the government and parliament currently have their seats in Erbil). Saddam had taken it from Kurdistan, and had been attempting to "Arabize" the area since the 1970s; first, by using economic incentives to encourage the transfer of teachers from other regions, and then by choosing Kirkuk as a place of exile for anyone who transgressed the orders of the party. The Turkmen, for their part, had always claimed to be the founders of Kirkuk, and now complain of discrimination by the Kurds. Since their arrival in the city, right after the American invasion, the Kurds have launched a hunt for Arabs: it's the ethnic cleansing of Saddam, only in reverse. Many Kurds have returned to reclaim their property, although the people living there often had nothing to do with the original expropriations organized by the dictator, which first laid the groundwork for the expulsion of the Kurds. Yet now, it's the current owners who must face the consequences. In the face of threats, many Arabs have sold or simply handed over their houses and returned to their native regions.

The key piece in play in Kirkuk is oil: 40 percent of Iraqi production is extracted from Kirkuk oil fields. In a preemptive move (and evidently with the backing of the U.S.), the Kurdish government has already signed contracts for the sale of oil, which the ministry in Baghdad is honoring, while awaiting the definition of the status of Kirkuk. The question has been put off till now (not even the Americans are disposed to cede complete control over the black gold of Kirkuk to the Kurds, although they owe a great deal to their most faithful allies). There's been talk of a referendum, which would further accelerate the ethnic cleansing, since the indigenous residents of Kirkuk include not only Kurds, but also Arabs (who have a strong presence in the province), Turkmen, Assyrians, and Chaldeans.

The Shiites, however, are against the federal state proposed by the Kurds, and since the January 2005 elections, it's the Shiites who dominate the government. But they are sensitive to the question of oil: the majority of Iraqi crude is produced in the south, and the Shiites claim that the old management, centralized in Baghdad, benefited only the capital and the central regions inhabited by Sunnis, who have no oil of their own. For this reason, they're willing to compromise on the question of federalism, as demonstrated in the text of the constitution ratified in August and backed by the October 15, 2005, referendum.

Federalism is not the only contested point between Shiites and Kurds—after all, it took three months just to form a government.

The slate that won the election, sponsored by al Sistani, is dominated by two religious parties: SCIRI, led by Abdelaziz al Hakim, and Dawa, led by Prime Minister Ibrahim al Jaafari. Both want an Islamic state, inspired by the Iranian model. Their spiritual guide is Iranian himself: although he has lived in Iraq for forty years (in Najaf), Ali al Sistani has kept his Iranian citizenship, which means he cannot even vote. But he was willing to proclaim a fatwa to make the Iraqis vote, a move that has little to do with democracy; neither does the proposed Islamic state he supports, for that matter. The champions of the "democratization" of Iraq must know this full well.

An Islamic state has its supporters among conservative Sunnis (Wahabbists) who do not, however, agree with the chosen "Iranian model," which has Shiite roots. The dismantling of the secular state worries laypeople of every sect, as well as the two major Kurdish parties, both supporters of the lay state. In the January 2005 elections, the Americans supported the Kurdish parties—overlooking cases of electoral fraud—in order to counter the Islamist Shiite landslide. They failed: the Shiite candidate backed by the U.S., ex-premier Iyad Allawi, got only 13.8 percent of the vote. The Kurds thus had to make concessions about relying on Islam as the principal source of law—the constitution actually creates a high court of religion to make certain that no law is contrary to shari'a—in order to obtain the backing of the Shiite religious parties on the issue of federalism. In the end, the Kurdish government was able to guarantee the ability to change any federal laws that conflict with local legislation. What's more, the new national constitution ratifies the laws handed down by the Kurdish government in its own constitution, written in 1992.

While Kurds and Shiites reached a compromise on the constitution to defend their reciprocal interests, conflict with the Sunni minority remains fierce, particularly around the issue of federalism—

based, above all, on the division of petroleum resources. The constitution states: "Oil and natural gas are the property of the entire Iraqi
people" (article 109). It adds: "The central government administers
oil and gas extracted from existing wells, together with the governments of the regions and provinces which produce them" (article
110). It speaks only of "functioning wells"—what about new ones?
There are also issues of compensation for the past use of oil resources on the horizon. It's easy to understand the concern of the
Sunnis, who would have no wells at all if Kirkuk were handed over to
Kurdistan. And in the name of federalism, the Kurdish government
will have control of the sixty thousand–man *peshmerga*, the Kurdish
militia.

Another point of conflict with the Sunnis is "de-Baathification,"
the procedure aimed at excluding followers of the former party from
all political and institutional posts, and redefining the Baath Party as
an organization that spreads racist propaganda and supports terrorism. The Sunnis, in light of the October 15 referendum, are searching for cross-boundary alliances with other skeptics of federalism,
such as the radical Shiite leader Muqtada al Sadr. Other opponents
include secularists and many women's associations. The transitional
law provided that a majority of two-thirds in two provinces could
defeat the constitution. It was an amendment designed to favor the
Kurds, but instead it became an electoral weapon in the hands of
those Sunnis who abstained from voting in January 2005.

"We ask the Iraqi people to participate in the referendum on the
constitution, and defeat it, demonstrating who is behind it and who
has shaped it in opposition to the will of the Iraqi people," declared
Sheikh Hareth al Dhari, secretary of the Association of the Ulema, in
an interview with Al Majd TV on August 28, 2005.

The Kurdish government won the right to change the laws of

Baghdad through constitutional discussions. The Shiite religious parties, with armed militias at their disposal, didn't have to wait. They simply imposed the rule of shari'a throughout all the areas of southern Iraq under their control. All behavior that didn't conform to the most rigid and conservative interpretation of the Koran was punished. The first victims were women, who had to change their dress and behavior. To enforce the abolition of alcohol, which continued to be sold in the last years of the Saddam regime but could no longer be consumed in public, liquor stores—mostly owned by Christians—were burned. Some proprietors died in the flames of their own stores, while others were killed outright. The majority of Christians were forced to leave Basra and the south and either move to Mosul—where the strongest Christian community has settled—or emigrate.

THE NEW ARMY IN THE CROSSHAIRS

The Sunnis, who boycotted the January 2005 election, and the Shiites, who voted, agree on one goal: the end of the occupation. The withdrawal of foreign troops is in fact, at least on paper, part of the platform of the victorious Shiite slate. It's the same goal, but through different strategies: the Sunnis are fighting an armed battle with U.S. troops that they cannot win—yet even the marines cannot defeat the guerrillas in the field. The Shiites are aiming instead at the conquest of power, so they can one day simply ask for, and obtain, the withdrawal of troops. According to the affirmations of the current Iraqi government (under U.S. tutelage), foreign troops will be asked to leave only when the Iraqis have full territorial control. The coalition governments take more or less the same position, which for some (including Italy) probably means military disengagement in return for some participation in oil revenues, besides the divvying up of reconstruction contracts. For others, the U.S. in particular, it means a reduction and redeployment of American troops to avoid further bloodshed, which is taking its toll on Bush's ratings in the polls.

The creation of a new Iraqi army and security force thus becomes a crucial point. What kind of military can be created in a country whose national unity has been sacrificed in the ashes of the Baathist regime? The dissolution of the army and the Baath Party, which had widespread control of the territory, were among the most tragic errors committed by the Americans upon their arrival in Baghdad. The country fell into chaos, and the loss of control over the borders allowed groups of terrorists to enter Iraq and transform the country into fertile ground on which to fight their jihad against the Western infidels.

Occupation forces have therefore assumed the work of rebuilding an Iraqi army. It's a tough job, not least because recruits are a prime target for al Zarqawi. He keeps slaughtering them, probably with a dual aim: to keep an Iraqi army from gaining territorial control, thus having a pretext for asking for the removal of "infidel" troops; and at the same time, to strike at the "apostate" Shiites. In fact, recruits in the south are essentially Shiites, while in the north they are largely Kurds, aside from a few Sunni officials rehabilitated from Saddam's army. The new assault troops are for the most part *peshmerga*, Kurdish fighters trained in Kurdistan to combat Saddam. It's only natural: the Kurds are the most faithful allies of the Americans, and their targets are the resistance strongholds in the so-called Sunni Triangle near the border with Kurdistan. Yet, if the *peshmerga* are in the front lines of the combat units, it's clear the army will never have the defense of a united Iraq as its goal. These units are in fact more loyal to the government in Erbil than to the one in Baghdad. What's more, no Kurdish minister, including the president, avails himself of the new national Iraqi security forces for personal protection—that is entrusted instead to specially trained *peshmerga*. The same goes for Shiite political figures—they protect themselves with their own party militia, which is more loyal to the mosques and Tehran than to the institutions of Baghdad.

In addition this intrinsic weakness, there is the corruption that permeates everything to do with the Iraqi army, its personnel, and weapons. In short, it is reasonable to doubt whether these troops can ever replace foreign forces. Even the trained and equipped coalition forces are unable to exert territorial control, as the constant bloody attacks they suffer have shown. The Iraqi armed forces, on the other hand, mainly consist of "phantom battalions": after training, many soldiers just go home, while officials continue to pocket the salaries of soldiers who have disappeared or who exist only on paper. "The United States maintains that the security forces can count on 150,000 Iraqis, but I doubt there are more than 40,000," declared Mahmud Othman, an Iraqi member of parliament, to a journalist from the *Guardian* (July 24, 2005). He also cited a flagrant case of corruption in military spending: the $300 million spent by the Ministry of Defense—with American involvement—to buy twenty-four military helicopters and other equipment from Poland that was then practically thrown away. The helicopters that arrived in Baghdad had been built twenty-eight years ago, and the manufacturer recommended junking them after twenty-five years! And this is no isolated case. Iraqi minister of defense Ali Allawi denounced another instance of fraud in September 2005, involving military spending that amounted to a billion dollars. This case involved not just the purchase of the Polish helicopters, but of armored shields that, as it turned out, could be pierced by one bullet from an AK-47, and American MP-5 machine guns, purchased for thirty-five hundred dollars apiece and replaced by an Egyptian model worth two hundred dollars. With equipment like this, the police are no match for better-armed guerrillas, not to speak of the terrorists. So why don't the Americans arm the Iraqi police? Because they don't trust them. In fact, they suspect them of conspiring with the resistance: the police force, as opposed to the military, includes Sunni ex-police officers and ex-officials of Saddam's army. The Americans' fears are not unfounded. During the attack on Falluja in November of 2004, for example, resistance groups simply picked up and moved to Mosul, meeting with no resistance from the Iraqi forces of order along the way. In the Sunni Triangle, the distrust between police and occupation forces is reciprocal, and there's been no shortage of bloody clashes. In Falluja, in September of 2003, the Americans killed eight Iraqi policemen, who happened to pass an American base as they chased down a stolen car. The inefficiency of the Iraqi military could constitute a pretext for the Americans to refuse to withdraw from the country.

CIVIL WAR

Among the tasks shared by the Shiite religious party militias—the al Badr Brigades and the rivals of the Jaish al Mahdi of Muqtada, many of whom have enrolled in the police force—is not only imposing Islamic order, but also hunting down ex-Baathists. It's a hunt that has already resulted in thousands of deaths: at least one thousand in Basra alone. Shortly after the fall of Saddam, in June of 2003, I went to Basra, where the hunt had already begun at the hands of a group calling itself "Islamic Vendetta." They had targeted supporters of the

Baathist regime, but also communists—who had reopened their headquarters—and the new mayor. Now it's the religious party militias, often under cover of the police force, that are directly responsible for an informal Baathist witch hunt. According to charges made by the American freelance journalist Steven Vincent, who was assassinated after his article on this topic appeared in the *New York Times* on July 31, 2005, the Basra executioners were driving around in a police car. Vincent had confirmation of the rumors flying around the city from a second lieutenant in the police force, who for obvious reasons preferred to remain anonymous: "Certain police officials are perpetrating hundreds of assassinations every month in Basra, mainly of ex-Baath Party members. He told me that there is a sort of 'death car': a white Toyota Mark II that circles the streets of the city, taking actions that have nothing to do with police work, at the behest of extremist religious groups." In fact, a majority of police force members belong to religious groups: "75 percent of the policemen are with Muqtada, he's a great man," an official told Steven Vincent. And so, in police headquarters—as in the streets everywhere—the images of religious leaders have replaced the omnipresent portraits of Saddam, making clear that the police are more loyal to the mosque than to the state. Steven Vincent had also denounced the fact that the British forces in control of Basra—forces that are supposed to be preparing Iraqi troops and police to take over once the British withdraw—are closing their eyes to what's happening. And thus, on the night of August 1, a police vehicle could make even a freelance American journalist vanish, only to be found dead the next morning. British troops were forced to open their eyes to the links between the police and the Shiite militias on September 19, 2005, however, when Iraqi police arrested two British soldiers dressed as Arabs and turned them over to Muqtada's militia, to which many of the police belong.

The British troops freed the two disguised soldiers by destroying the building where they were held, and in the process provoked a rebellion. The victims of these Shiite executioners are mostly Sunni, and they have also been chased out of the university. Many have sold their houses and moved to Baghdad, where they may well be no safer. The Shiite death squads (linked to Interior Minister Bayan Jabr, a leader of the SCIRI and the Badr Brigades) are accused of assassinating many Sunni religious figures. The accusations are taken seriously by Prime Minister al Jaafari himself (also a Shiite). Over the last months, charges of maltreatment and murder of Sunnis by police special forces have grown, particularly after the discovery of eleven Sunni corpses, tortured and killed with a single bullet to the back of the head. All eleven, including an imam, had been arrested during a police raid north of Baghdad at dawn on July 10, 2005. "It's not the first time this has happened: we want to know who is responsible for these crimes," said Adnan al Dulaimi, head of the Sunni religious organization Waqf, while asking for an official inquiry into the case. During the same period, a commando unit made up mostly of Shiites launched a raid on Yarmuk Hospital in Baghdad, seizing thirteen Sunnis accused of being insurgents. Sixteen hours later, the bodies of ten of them were dropped off at the morgue. The hapless prisoners had been locked in an armored police wagon at temperatures approaching 122 degrees Fahrenheit, and had suffocated.

Rather than preventing civil war, the police—made up predominantly of Kurds and Shiites—are helping foment it. While civil war is often cited as the terrible alternative facing Iraq if foreign troops were to withdraw, it is already a reality, one materializing under the troops' distracted gaze. This reality is so evident that speaking of civil war is no longer taboo, even for the American ambassador in Baghdad, Zalmay Khalilzad. In mid-July, Khalilzad replaced Negroponte, who had always preferred to skate over the issue. Even so, the ex-ambassador to Kabul speaks of civil war as something the U.S. must do everything to avoid.

THE IRANIAN VICTORY

The significance of the electoral victory of the Shiite religious forces, sponsored by the Ayatollah Ali al Sistani, reaches far beyond the borders of Iraq: it has basically created the conditions for the birth of a second Shiite state, allied with Iran. Even if the "Iranian model" should fail to win over both secular resistance and fundamentalist Sunnis, who consider the Shiite schism a betrayal, the Iranian presence in Iraq and its political influence are already a reality. The leaders of the SCIRI—the al Hakim brothers, of whom only Abdelaziz has survived after his more charismatic brother, Mohammed Baqer, was assassinated in Najaf on August 29, 2003—spent years in exile in Tehran, as guests of the Iranian regime. It was the Iranian Revolutionary Guards who trained the Badr Brigades, the armed wing of the SCIRI, to fight against Saddam, taking on the task of interrogating—and torturing—the Iraqis taken prisoner by the Iranians during the Iran-Iraq war. If the prisoners refused to renounce Saddam, the treatment reserved for them did not respect the Geneva Conventions, to put it mildly; if, instead, they "repented," they were enrolled directly in the brigades. Many prisoners were Shiites because Saddam used them as cannon fodder in the fight against their Iranian brethren. Around ten thousand men of the Badr Brigades returned to Iraq with their leaders after the fall of Saddam. Theoretically, they should have come disarmed, but they did not, and their numbers grew as the months passed. Among their counselors are Iranian militiamen from across the border. Even the radical Muqtada draws inspiration from the holy Iranian city of Qom. The first Iraqi religious party, Dawa (founded in 1957 to oppose the influence of the Communist Party, which then represented the majority of the Shiite community), also has many Iranian friends.

The Baghdad government not only aspires to an Iranian template; it also actively defends the interests of Tehran. The SCIRI leader Abdelaziz al Hakim has proposed a payment of millions of dollars to Iran in war reparations, a choice in stark contrast with Washington's attempts to have Saddam's international debts forgiven. Among the projects of the Iraqi minister of oil, Ibrahim Bahr al Ulum (a Shiite), is construction of an oil pipeline that would connect Basra and the Iranian port of Abadan. But the most surprising aspect of the new relations between Iraq and Iran is the treaty for military cooperation, underwritten on July 7, 2005, in Tehran by the two ministers of defense, the Iraqi Saadoun al Dulaimi and the Iranian Mohammed Najjar. Among other areas, the accord covers military training—a section of the agreement that may have to wait to be realized, since it would be quite an unusual phenomenon if American and Iranian soldiers were to find themselves side by side, training Iraqi troops, at the same time that the U.S. is threatening Iran over its nuclear ambitions. The partnership might be particularly uneasy, given the former position of the new Iranian Minister of Defense, Mohammed Najjar: he was the first commander of the Middle Eastern Revolutionary Guards, where he was engaged in exporting the Islamic revolution and supporting the activities of pro-Iranian groups. In his first address to the Majlis (the advisory council to the Iranian Parliament), Najjar affirmed that he would dedicate particular attention to the "production of effective tools for asymmetric warfare."

Collaboration between the two countries is already in place at the intelligence level. Iranian alliances in Iraq, since the time of Saddam, were not limited to "natural" ties with the Shiites, but reached all the way to the Patriotic Union of Kurdistan. Current President Jalal Talabani and his followers took refuge in Iran when they fled Saddam's repression. It's no coincidence that during the inauguration of the Kurdish Parliament, an Iranian intelligence officer was quoted in *Le Monde Diplomatique* as saying: "The men we have supported are now in power."

But why did Bush encourage the allies of Tehran to take power? Another miscalculation? Sheer blindness? "America today, after the failure of its undertaking in Iraq, wants to realize immediate profits that favor Bush and his administration. Bush doesn't care what will happen later, once he leaves the White House," says Sheikh Hareth al Dhari, of the Association of the Ulema. He adds: "Bush and his men show no consideration for American interests. Otherwise, they would have explained the failure of their enterprise to their people and withdrawn their forces from the country" (from an interview with Al Majd TV, August 28, 2005). Bush is certainly not looking after the interests of the United States, much less those of Iraq. With the profound fault lines provoked by the occupation and the efforts at ethnic/sectarian partition, Iraq is poised on the brink of Lebanese-style polarization and dissolution. In this situation, one incident is enough to push it over—in Beirut it was the 1975 Falangist attack on a bus and the massacre of twenty-seven Palestinians on board. And there is no lack of such incidents in Iraq, nor is there a shortage of far worse incidents, such as the carnage at the Kadhimiya Mosque. And yet, today when you ask someone in Baghdad whether he is Shiite or Sunni, the proud response is still: "I'm Iraqi." For how much longer?

NINE

THE ACCIDENT

VARIOUS SENSATIONS are superimposed, one over another. I still don't feel free; I'm infected by the tension and disquiet of my "liberators." We're not safe yet—we have to make it to the airport. I can't manage to shake the terror accumulated during the month of captivity, and the tense wait of a few moments before. Nicola Calipari, who sits in the back of the car with me to make me feel more secure, tries to put me at ease. He has me take the cotton off my eyes, and remove the shawl wrapped around my head, which I always find oppressive. "You're free now," he repeats, sensing, evidently, that it's difficult for me to grasp. Then he calls his boss, the director of SISMI (Italian Security and Military Service), General Pollari. I don't know what to say other than "thank you." I feel fine, but just as I did at times during my captivity, I don't feel completely inside my own body, as though I can't quite put my feet on the ground. Nicola tries to get another line to Italy so I can talk to Pier or Gabriele Polo (the editor in chief of *Il Manifesto*)—maybe by now they'll have already arrived at Palazzo Chigi, the seat of the Italian prime minister. But the call won't go through and he throws the phone on the front seat. The driver, meanwhile, has been on the phone since we left—calling whom, I don't know—to say that we're arriving at the airport, "all three of us." And just as I begin to grasp that I'm no longer a prisoner—the agent at the wheel, who knows Baghdad well, says we're only a mile from the airport—shots interrupt my emotional tumult.

"They're attacking us, they're attacking us!" yells the agent. But who is attacking us? Who could it be? We left my abductors twenty minutes ago and they can't possibly have followed us. They could never have entered this American-controlled zone. And I can't imagine it's the Americans spraying us with machine-gun fire. They've surely been alerted to our arrival—in the days following that will be confirmed. And yet, it's them. It's the famous "friendly fire," with effects no less devastating than enemy fire. While the driver, who is on the phone with General Pollari, continues to scream that we're with the Italian Embassy, Calipari throws me down. I end up wedged between the driver's seat and my own, and he covers me with his body to protect me. The shots are coming, in fact, from the right, the side he's sitting on, along with a beam of light. Calipari must have been hit right away, because he never says another word. Andrea Carpani—this is the name of the driver, which I only learn upon my return to Italy—is yelling, while Nicola is silent. I'm terrified—the car is being bombarded with bullets. Perhaps it's my terror that makes the shots seem far more numerous than they are in reality.

When the shooting stops, the agent at the wheel gets out of the car, still on the phone, yelling "We're with the Italian Embassy!" while soldiers draw near and surround him. I can't move. I'm paralyzed with anguish. Why doesn't Nicola speak? I don't dare imagine what's happened. But his body grows heavier on top of mine, and when I manage to shift him, I hear a death rattle. He's dying, he's dead! No! The man who freed me is dead, and he died to protect me. It's as though my freedom has ended just as it was about to begin. All my emotions freeze in that moment. It's a terrible sensation to feel a person die on top of you, as though a part of you dies as well. And in fact, after that rain of gunfire I can't tell whether I'm alive and imagining I'm dead, or already dead and just imagining I'm alive.

The soldiers who fired on us arrive: they open Nicola's door and raise his head. "Shit!" one of them says. They seem surprised, but not frightened. They're young. But they can't be that inexperienced: it will come out at the inquest that almost all of them are officers, except for two specialists, an unusual makeup for a platoon of this type.

Once they've verified that Calipari is dead, they come over to my side to pull me out. I can't move by myself. It's only then that I realize I've been wounded. I feel blood dripping, but I hadn't even felt the bullet that tore through my left shoulder. And yet it was big, 7.62 millimeters (according to the military commission's report), and besides ripping away a piece of muscle (the deltoid), leaving a hole that measured four centimeters in diameter, it fractured the shoulder bone in passing, filling me with bone splinters. The soldiers pull me out and lay me down on the pavement. They start cutting away everything I'm wearing—overcoat, sweatshirt, T-shirt—searching for the wound. I stay like that on the ground, naked to the waist, for at least a quarter of an hour, until a vehicle comes to take me to the hospital. I'm at some distance from Andrea, who is confronting the soldiers; they have him surrounded with weapons drawn. From the ground, I see a military truck off the side of the road, in a field around forty to fifty feet away. It's the Humvee they were shooting from. A soldier comes over holding an IV, which he tries uselessly to insert in the vein of my right arm, the only one usable. After breaking several veins, leaving my hand and arm covered in bruises for days, he gives up. ("The needle was too big," I later read in the report.) Suddenly I feel a terrible thirst. I ask for water, but they tell me to wait because I'll be taken to the hospital at any minute. I can't wait. I can't breathe; I feel my throat closing. I'm suffocating. A bottle of water arrives and they give me a drop, but it's not enough to let me catch my breath. I hear Agent Carpani in the distance asking how I am, but I can't manage to signal to him. He calms down when he sees me rise and get in the vehicle that will take me to the hospital, the same Humvee they were shooting from. He'll be taken to the hospital, too—he's wounded in one arm—but I won't meet him there. It doesn't take long—fifteen minutes, they tell me—to get to the hospital, although the Humvee doesn't go above ten kilometers an hour.

We're not far from the international zone and when I arrive at the American military hospital I feel like I'm entering the set of the television show *ER*. It's not the first time in Iraq that I find myself in a situation stranger than fiction, but for me, this time is the most dramatic. Immediately, I ask them to call the Italian ambassador; he lives in the Green Zone and doesn't take long to arrive. Meanwhile, I'm assaulted by a group of doctors and nurses pulling at me from all sides. A nurse takes off the chain my kidnappers gave me. They give me oxygen, then begin the standard exams. From an X-ray, they can see instantly that my left lung is collapsing. Two bullet fragments are touching the pleura, and the lung is deflating. That's why I can't breathe! They bombard me with a hail of questions, and since some of their accents are particularly impenetrable, at first I don't respond. So they send me a doctor who speaks Serbo-Croatian! They finally grasp that they just need to speak a little slower to be understood; on top of everything else, I'm in shock. They check that there are no other contraindications to giving me general anesthesia. First, however, I manage to see Ambassador Gianludovico De Martino, who has me speak on the phone to Gianni Letta, the undersecretary to the Italian prime minister. Then, as they wheel me into the operating room, someone draws near, and asks from behind my back—I can't see his face—if I'm the journalist who had been abducted. The question is unsettling: until now they had only asked my name and nationality, although evidently they must have known who I was. Now I'm in their hands—I certainly can't hide my identity. After all, they are our allies, but after what just happened, that fact doesn't reassure me at all. I have no choice: I must be operated on to be able to leave.

I wake from the anesthesia in a recovery room. I'm sitting up in bed (I'll have to sleep like this for almost a month in order to drain the liquid from my lung). I'm surrounded by IV towers: one with an antibiotic, another to prevent infection from the bullet—this is the greatest danger, the doctors in Italy will tell me—then morphine, another for hydration, and others for I don't know what, all feeding into a kind of valve that's directly connected to my aorta. Another valve is located on my femoral artery, just in case. When a liquid pouch runs out, it lets out a whistle, which quickly becomes unbearable if the nurse on duty doesn't come and replace it right away. I can't move. My left arm is imprisoned in a cast because of the broken shoulder, and I'm tethered by oxygen tubes, the IVs, etc.

They had said they would come to get me around five o'clock in the morning, but in that uncomfortable position, with aches and pain everywhere, the hours drag. Without even a watch, I have no perception of time. I should be used to it. Then I hear a commotion. The first to arrive is the ambassador with a few agents. He tells me Pier is at the airport. I can't imagine he came all the way to Baghdad—he must mean the airport in Rome, I think—and so when Pier shows up with the other agents who will take me back to Italy, I am truly surprised. Finally, a pleasant surprise! Although in these conditions, I can't even show my joy.

The preparations for my departure are lengthy. Given my precarious medical condition, an American doctor was prepared to accompany me—and from what I could understand, he wouldn't have minded taking a quick trip to Italy to escape the nightmare in Baghdad—but the team that arrives from Italy includes a doctor, and the American has to put off his transfer. In the end, everything is ready by 5:30 a.m. I have only to sign a receipt to get back the few belongings I had with me at the moment I was shot, things gathered by the soldiers on the scene. The gold chain, however, is missing—they took it off the night before and they can't find it. I tell them to look for it—why should I leave it to the Americans? I insist out of obstinacy, more than anything else. At a certain point I think I hear a voice saying they found it, but it's not on the list they give me, nor in the plastic bag—one of the black ones you use for garbage—where everything has been thrown in higgledy-piggledy. The black shawl, which had become a bit like Linus's blanket, is also missing. I'm really sorry for that. The chain I give up for lost, but after returning home, I find it, by pure chance—it is hidden inside a shoe that I hadn't touched since the moment I was wounded.

After the transfer to the airport by helicopter, at seven o'clock we take off. This time, Baghdad truly fades into the distance, although I can't even raise my head to look out the window. I'm laid out in the back of the prime minister's airplane, hampered by the drainage mechanism for my lung, and any movement makes me vomit. I'm used to the unusual method of Baghdad takeoffs and landings, designed to avoid attack. You arrive at high altitude over the city, and then spiral down at headlong speed. At takeoff, you have to reach cruising altitude almost immediately. But given my condition, the plane cannot fly at the normal high altitude, so it takes five and a half hours to get to Rome, two more than it took on the flight into Baghdad. I land in Rome exhausted, but finally home—although, in reality, I would only set foot in my own house after spending three weeks in the Celio military hospital.

Celio was entirely new to me. They had first told me they would take me to the Gemelli Hospital, but given the coincidental hospitalization of the pope at that facility, my additional presence would have overloaded the hospital with media attention. I had heard of Celio from friends who'd passed through during their military service, many years ago, and had preserved only bad memories of the place. Being hospitalized in a military facility seemed, above all, ill suited to a pacifist; although I did figure it must be the best place to treat bullet wounds. Yet I would have to rethink my feelings about the military hospital. Celio was another of those involuntary positive discoveries I made because of my misadventure: not only because of the efficiency and professionalism of the care, but also because of the humanity and solidarity with which they surrounded me, protecting me from the press and the excessive flood of friends and acquaintances (whom I would have seen willingly, had I only been in condition to do so).

My arrival in Italy was painfully marked by the death of Calipari, a person whom I knew for only twenty minutes, but whose extraordinary character was immediately apparent. This impression was confirmed in Italy, first by Gabriele and Pier who had met with him during my captivity, then by his wife Rosa, his colleagues, and others who had known him in earlier years, particularly when he worked at the Bureau of Immigration. In fact, he was immediately celebrated as a national hero, not only by the authorities, but also by ordinary people. I'm not a fan of rhetorical definitions, but Calipari and his companions gave me a new image of people who choose to "serve their country" (still not a particularly apt characterization). However you define him, a person like Calipari cannot be allowed to die with impunity, without everything possible being done to discover the truth of what happened in Baghdad on the night of March 4 (as even the President of the Republic, Carlo Azeglio Ciampi, has requested). In this, the government and the authorities who celebrated him as a hero should take the lead—they have the power, for example, to insist that American authorities respond to the requests of the Italian judiciary. It won't be easy, because the Americans are denying the truth—and they are the only ones who know exactly what happened.

After presenting contrasting versions of the facts, the American military inquest ended, predictably, with the full absolution of the soldiers who fired on us. Calipari case closed. The U.S. military version held that our vehicle was speeding (forty to fifty miles an hour), did not stop at repeated signals—voice, warning lights, and shots fired in the air—and thus the soldiers were forced to fire to stop the car. The version of the two Italian witnesses—Agent Carpani and I, which coincided substantially, although we never spoke—maintains the contrary: the car was not speeding at all (twenty-five to thirty-five miles an hour), and there was no warning to stop. The car was illuminated with a warning beacon simultaneously as shots were fired, not before, and it was hit from the right and at the height of the passengers, not in the motor—which was hit only once—or in the tires, as might be expected if soldiers were shooting to stop the vehicle.

This latter version was also supported by the Italian government, at the insistence of Foreign Minister Gianfranco Fini, when he reported to parliament on the incident. The attitude of the Italian government spurred the Americans, who had already settled the matter by labeling it a banal "accident," to nominate an investigative military commission, which included—in an unusual concession—two Italian representatives: the diplomatic advisor to Palazzo Chigi, Ambassador Cesare Ragaglini, and the SISMI general Pierluigi Campregher. Both were relegated to the rank of simple observers, however, since they could not directly intervene in the investigation. Moreover, when the two Italians arrived in Baghdad on March 12, all the evidence at the scene of the shooting had been erased: the car had been removed, along with the bullets, because, the Americans said, they might give passing military vehicles a flat tire! I was interrogated twice by the commission, led by General Peter Vangjel—once in writing and once via videoconferencing with Baghdad—apparently without my testimony being given any weight at all. The only thing that seemed to worry the general was the correlation between my testimony and that of Agent Carpani. Perhaps that's why the American report cites only the testimony of Carpani, which was harder to ignore. The commission was nominated on March 8, and concluded its work with a report made public on April 30, 2005. That report, however, was not accepted by the two Italian representatives, who edited another version, with a completely different slant. Of course, the Americans confirmed their own version—despite the often contradictory testimony of the soldiers who were part of the mobile checkpoint, some of which cast doubt on the account of the only soldier who, according to the U.S. version, had fired. Everything in order, in other words. The immunity of American soldiers is protected once again. The Americans justify this position, arrogantly, with the argument that in Iraq, they're fighting a war—a war that Bush had declared over and done with on May 1, 2003, on the deck of the aircraft carrier *Lincoln*!

Beyond the claims of the soldiers, who said they signaled their presence and requests to halt with light beacons, shots fired in the air, etc.—claims that are completely false—one fact that comes out of both the American and Italian reports is particularly unsettling. Starting shortly before 8 p.m., and every few minutes thereafter, the commander of the mobile patrol, Captain Drew, repeatedly asked the Infantry Battalion Tactical Operation Center (TOC) if he can stand down roadblock 541. "The captain in charge of the company declared his concern over leaving his soldiers in a static position for more than fifteen minutes, thus exposing them to possible attacks," one reads in the reports. But he is continually told to hold his position, until the last telephone call, the seventh in half an hour, placed at 8:30 p.m., when he was not only ordered to hold his position, but told: "Division C directed us not to leave the roadblock because the convoy would be passing on the Irish Route within around twenty minutes." The convoy referred to—identified only after blacked-out sections of the report were revealed—belonged to Negroponte.

The ex-American ambassador in Baghdad never moved except by helicopter and was afraid to set foot outside his own building (a former palace of Saddam's) even for a photo opportunity, as a photographer friend of mine told me. Yet that night, since bad weather precluded the use of a helicopter, he had decided to go to dinner at Camp Victory by car, and to do so, had blocked off the road that we would be using. But the cordon, when we arrived, had already been removed because Negroponte had reached his destination. "The VIP convoy left the international zone with four Humvees at approximately 7:45. It arrived at the entrance to Camp Victory at 8:10. The convoy reached its destination at Camp Victory at 8:20," reads the U.S. report. In fact, the convoy had traveled by another road, and returned by helicopter, since by then it had stopped raining. Negroponte's escort transmitted all this information. But "there is no evidence to show that the artillery battalion transmitted the information about the VIP's time of departure and arrival to other units," underlines the Italian report. Moreover, by 8:30, the agent at the wheel of our car had already communicated that we were on our way, and would be arriving, oddly enough, in just "about twenty minutes" after the last communication to Captain Drew. He had spoken to the official Italian liaison, General Mario Marioli, vice commandant of the armed multinational forces, who was in continual contact with the American cocommander, Captain Green.

Could the division chief, who had repeatedly told Drew to hold his position, really have been ignorant of the fact that Negroponte had already arrived at his destination? Surely he wasn't informed that Negroponte would pass at 8:50 on the Irish Route, because that was false. So why was mistaken information passed on to the commander of the mobile patrol? And what effect did that information have? If we grant that it was not a cover for something we don't know, and will probably never know, at the very least this false information served to create a climate in which the "accident" became almost inevitable. Because the soldiers, already stressed by their long wait, were expecting Negroponte's convoy at exactly that moment; and when they saw an Iraqi car arrive instead, they didn't think twice before shooting, without warning or verification, just as they do all the time.

The rules of engagement for these roadblocks are unknown, since you're dealing with uncodified "missions" with no written orders. Procedure is thus entrusted to the divisions themselves. At headquarters, investigators found no trace of that particular roadblock's "duty logs": they were destroyed at the end of every duty shift (which is totally illegal). In fact, in jargon, these roadblocks are defined by Westerners as "illegal checkpoints," since they are not marked and no one knows the rules of engagement. The justification for the lack of road signs alerting travelers to the presence of roadblock 541 by the U.S. official responsible was pathetic: passengers in vehicle traffic wouldn't have understood the significance of any signs, he said, since they were written in Arabic and English (and said things like "Stop," "Slow Down," and "Danger"). And anyway, signs weren't available to that unit because "for a few weeks they were in the hands of technicians who were supposed to tape over certain parts and phrases considered offensive to civilians." (!) After all, the operative second-in-command had responded to a specific question about his consideration for the safety of civilians by saying: "Everything is dangerous in Iraq."

In this way, Iraqis are killed in Baghdad every day, without their deaths even making news—unlike the victims of car bombs.

The lack of respect for civilians at these "illegal" roadblocks, underlined in the report edited by the two Italian members of the U.S. military commission, is in sharp contrast to the American approach, in which any use of force is justified by the fact that soldiers in Iraq are acting in a state of war. And this state of war, as witnessed by two representatives of the Italian government, points up the incongruity of the Italian presence in Iraq, which is marketed at home as a "mission of peace." If such a report came from the Italian government itself, the logical consequence would have been the withdrawal of the troops—yet that wasn't even taken into consideration. On the contrary, the Italian government reaffirmed its alliance with Bush, despite the fact that the U.S. had closed the Calipari case, while the Italian report basically reopened it on the basis of the Italian testimony (Carpani's and mine).

The ball then passed to the Italian judiciary, which almost two months after the incident, managed to have the Toyota Corolla in which we were riding at the moment of the shooting sent to Italy to be examined. The car arrived on April 27, when leaks about the U.S.

military commission's report were already circulating. The first reports by the experts who examined the car indicated that it could not have been only one soldier who fired. This by itself demolishes the American report. In any case, although the names of the soldiers who made up the mobile patrol are known, thanks to the uncensoring of blacked-out areas, Italy can never proceed against them, since they are covered by immunity while operating overseas. Thanks to international accords, in fact, American soldiers can only be tried in the United States. And the Vangjel Commission has already absolved these particular soldiers.

How far does the Italian judiciary have the fortitude or the means to go? Much will depend on political will. Precedents like the Cermis case, in which a NATO jet struck a cable car line at a ski resort at Mount Cermis in 1998, causing the deaths of twenty people, don't give much cause for optimism. Time is also pressing, and the Italian investigation has to conclude by March. [It was in fact concluded in January 2006, when the judiciary authority in Rome declared it closed. The only U.S. soldier named as a suspect in the investigation was Mario Lozano, a member of the New York Army National Guard. Lozano could not be located and did not respond to the charges against him. The U.S. government refused to respond to Italian requests for the names of other soldiers involved in the shooting.] But "peace is not possible without justice," as Rosa Calipari wrote in a piece about her husband's death for the Italian newspaper *L'Unità* on August 31, 2005.

TEN

ITALY

IMMEDIATELY AFTER my kidnapping, when I saw the announcement of the abduction made with such unusual timeliness on Iraqi television, I began asking myself how Pier and my family would be told and what effect it would have on them. Surely ANSA, the Italian wire service, would have spread the news instantly, given that I was supposed to be at lunch with the ANSA correspondent and other colleagues when I was seized. Even Iraqya TV was already showing my picture when it reported the news. At my newspaper, *Il Manifesto*, the news would certainly have arrived almost in real time, right before the morning editorial meeting. These were among the many questions that could only be answered upon my return.

The first colleague to read the wire dispatch to *Il Manifesto* was so shocked that he couldn't manage to tell anyone. Pier found out while he was working in his office, from a friend who had watched the noon broadcast of the RAI Channel 3 news. Other colleagues at the paper confirmed the information, and Pier then had the thankless task of telling my mother, and she, in turn, the rest of my family. Often during my imprisonment I had tried to imagine the possible reactions in Italy: of Pier, of my family, of colleagues, of friends, and of public opinion. But even using all my possible powers of imagination, I couldn't begin to re-create what was actually happening outside my prison—and not only in Italy, but all over the world. That's a puzzle I have been piecing together over the past months, through conversations, images, and writings, but above all, by talking it over with Pier.

This is how Pier remembers that day, Friday, February 4:

"At that moment, a film began in which I had always dreaded playing a role. Until then I had only imagined such a scenario—maybe to ward off bad luck. Certainly abduction had always been a possibility, which I inevitably thought about every time you left on a trip. I feel like the sensation was stronger the last time, but that's almost certainly hindsight. Or maybe the memory of how you'd squeaked by three or four times before (in Somalia, Afghanistan, Iraq) made me feel that sooner or later something was bound to happen. Right after getting the news, I thought about everyone I needed to inform, and how I'd do it. I called my parents and your parents before they could see it on the one o'clock news. Then I started an endless series of interviews about you: who you were, highlights of your work.... *Il Manifesto* held a press conference: everyone was asking for your photo. The next day, I went to the conference of the DS [the Party of the Democratic Left] to participate in a debate, but I also wanted to ask the DS leaders for their opinion, and get some advice on whom to contact and whom I could trust. The first contacts with Gianni Letta and SISMI were made by Valentino Parlato [one of the founding editors of *Il Manifesto*] and Gabriele Polo. I only met [Letta and the SISMI agents] during the next phase, when negotiations were already launched. Beginning on Saturday, we started meeting at the newspaper to discuss and evaluate the news and events coming out of Iraq, and to decide what actions to take the next day. In the evening we'd wait for the call from Palazzo Chigi, which could just be "goodnight," or "come on over," if there was news or questions to discuss. During the day, it was a matter of managing the requests for information or interviews that came from media sources all over the world, and receiving the visits of politicians and envoys of all stripes. These visits were acts of real solidarity, not just courtesy calls, marked by the common conviction that we had to do everything possible to obtain your liberation, without neglecting any hypothesis or possible channel of communication. On this point, figures of both the center-right and center-left were united.

"The idea of a national demonstration came up immediately and sprang—you could say—from an objective demand for action that was growing not only in the peace movement, but also in vast tracts of public opinion (which at other times had not been particularly sympathetic to pacifist themes). Furthermore—and this is a crucial point—we were disposed to believe in the political nature of the abduction, or better, the political motivation of the group of kidnappers. This conviction was confirmed by SISMI, as well as by Arab journalists with Gulf television stations, who are generally well informed, and by political and institutional forces in Arab countries that had been close to the Baath Party. So once we'd excluded the possibility of a terrorist network or a simple criminal act, we were faced with a challenge that was political in nature, and to which we had to respond on the same level—and not only with pacifist and humanitarian themes, which was the position more or less taken by the government: 'You should free her because she's a pacifist and a friend of the Iraqi people' (Foreign Minister Gianfranco Fini). We therefore planned a political response on every possible level. I willingly participated in various television and radio broadcasts, and though it was difficult, I tried to avoid the sentimental or humanitarian angle—backed by the opinion of a huge majority of Italians, I insisted instead on criticizing the politics of war and of Italy's role in the Bush/Blair campaign. This was the basis of our slogan: 'Free Giuliana and all the Iraqis.' We were pressing for the withdrawal of the troops, not because you'd been kidnapped, but because it was the right policy for our government to follow—particularly after the Iraqi elections in January of 2005, when the U.S.-backed candidate, the only one to support the long-term presence of foreign troops, got only 13 percent of the vote, while the candidates that made withdrawal part of their platform were victorious. In this spirit I participated in dozens of debates and interviews, often with Gabriele Polo. I made myself available for everything, because I felt it could be useful. After your first video was broadcast, an audience member reproached me during a show for political speechifying when I should have been begging for your freedom. I replied that you had asked me to do exactly what I was doing, and I found the figure of the husband begging for his companion's freedom both useless and pathetic. Naturally, we solicited these television appearances, as well as the visits from politicians and the messages—in particular those from the President of the Republic and the pope—but they also sprang from an authentic participation and wish to help on the part of the media and other institutions. I was frankly amazed at this willingness to help. I didn't expect such widespread and firm support—aside from the usual exceptions—for the arguments we were making for your liberation, which was also, at heart, support for your professional choices. That changed a bit after your liberation, however."

My abductors, as you had guessed, were highly sensitive to the mobilization for my liberation. I was particularly surprised by their excite-

ment over the soccer captains wearing jerseys that said "Free Giuliana" ... particularly since Totti (the Italian soccer star) wore one too, and one of my abductors was a huge fan of his. How did you get the idea?

"In reality, when we contacted Franco Carraro, president of Federcalcio [the Italian federation of professional soccer teams], the initial idea was to ask if we could display 'Free Giuliana' banners in all the stadiums. That led to the jerseys that all the team captains wore before the start of each game."

The only demonstration I could see from my prison was the one at the Campidoglio (the capital buildings in Rome). It had a big effect on me, seeing my portrait hanging there, the people holding candles in the square. It fed my courage, and gave me the impression that I wasn't alone or abandoned. This was the first demonstration, the day after my abduction.

"As early as Friday, Walter Veltroni [the current mayor of Rome] had called me, and the idea of the vigil was born, but it wasn't—it couldn't be—a big, militant demonstration. I had some concerns about the subsequent march on February 19, for the same reason: the fear that it would become a rally for political parties and militants. Among other issues, a few center-left politicians raised a real doubt: as we mobilized the public for your freedom, we ran the risk of simply raising the ransom price, of upping the value of the hostage in the kidnappers' eyes, when it may have been better to keep a low profile on the whole situation. I have to admit that at the beginning—maybe out of fear—I was susceptible to this concern. It was Valentino Parlato who cut straight to the heart of the matter: "This is a political abduction. A greater dose of politics serves to strengthen Giuliana's position and make her abductors understand that it's an error on their part to silence a voice like hers." Of course, we were betting on the fact that the abductors had a political sensibility—if they were just bandits, none of this would have made any sense.

"Once we'd guessed at the political nature of the abduction, it naturally followed that raising the political level of our response would serve to facilitate the negotiations and make the abductors understand that it would be counterproductive for them to take the abduction to extreme consequences. With the demonstration, we were responding to a demand that came not only from the peace movement, [but from the public at large], as the reaction to your first video confirmed. I remain convinced that the video was the key that doubled popular participation. It pulled ordinary people into the streets: the video brought out the positive emotions often missing in our country. It might be worth reflecting on this: you can't explain the massive mobilization of people that followed your abduction just by the symbolic value of your plight. There wasn't the same reaction to other cases, before or after. Certainly, your affiliation with *Il Manifesto*, and your long, well-defined political history, played an important part, by expanding the circle of those who knew and esteemed you, but it's not enough to explain what happened. I believe many people saw you as a positive symbol of a number of things: a woman; a conscientious, professional, yet combative journalist, not a prima donna; not overbearing in debates; in short, a normal person, capable but fragile, because the video underlined your fragility. All of that contributed to creating a symbol. It's a bit like a cormorant swimming in an oil slick: hundreds of cormorants die in the same way, just as hundreds of children die of hunger, and then suddenly, one of them becomes the center of attention—a symbol, an icon. Why? For many reasons: because of the way the media select and distribute news; because people need to release the good they have inside and pour it into something worth believing in; because they need a motive to pull them out into the streets. Or maybe there is no reason: it just happens and that's it. Whatever the reason, there were longtime peace activists at the February 19 demonstration, but also lots of ordinary people who had never been to an antiwar demonstration in their lives."

But did this mobilization provoke a change of heart in ordinary people on the issue of the war, on the situation in Iraq?

"It forced people to reflect. It shifted something. The majority of people in this country probably don't correspond to the picture often painted of "Berlusconian," don't-give-a-damn Italians. Most people aren't like that, but they hide their better qualities, they're fearful, and your plight served to prick their consciences, by offering them a good reason to express themselves and to demonstrate. And it put the issue of the war in Iraq front and center. Because seeing the news on television is one thing, but the abduction of a person—even if you don't know her personally—forces you to ask what is really going on in Iraq.

"Naturally, it wasn't like this for everyone: some newspapers expressed the views of the 'other Italy,' and had no scruples about mocking or taking advantage of your situation, both before and after [your liberation]. But this is simply the other side of what we were saying earlier.

"It's also worth noting that during the demonstration there were no slogans criticizing Berlusconi and Bush—not because the demonstrators were uncritical, but because that wasn't the goal. We were asking the government to take its cue from the changed reality in Iraq, and send a strong political signal by scheduling the withdrawal of the troops. All this was going on while we—*Il Manifesto* and I—were keeping the closest of ties with the Berlusconi administration and SISMI, with no tension at all. Each of us was just doing his job. We believed the Italian government's policy of negotiation was the right thing to do, and on their part, Letta—who represented the Italian government—did not disapprove of our initiatives, including the demonstration. So there was a parallel policy: on our part, mobilization against the war, for your freedom and the freedom of all Iraqis; on the government's part, the policy of negotiation and international political pressure for the liberation of a woman who was both a pacifist and a friend to the Iraqi people.

"I'd like to recall two things from those days that I think best describe the climate at the time and offer an interesting viewpoint from which to understand the underlying mood of this country.

"A few days after your first video was released, we had the idea of publishing a letter I wrote to you and your abductors in *Il Manifesto,* in both Italian and Arabic, in the hopes that it might somehow reach you in your prison and serve to keep attention focused on your case.

"It began like this: 'Dear Giuliana, in the video you seemed to me like a caged bird...'(*Il Manifesto*, February 22, 2005).

"This had an unimaginable effect—not in Iraq, naturally, but here. In dozens of schools, children wrote about [the letter], and drew pictures of this image of the caged bird. Many sent their work to *Il Manifesto*, and you were able to see it when you returned. Clearly, their teachers had given the assignment, but that wasn't the point. The [children's work] represented a shared emotion: their drawings and words expressed in simple form what we were all thinking. I would love to publish them somehow.

"The other thing was the willingness to help on the part of those in the entertainment and news businesses. Don't get me wrong: I know perfectly well that in those days you were big news; you, your parents, and me too, in some ways. So there was a professional interest in inviting us, and having us speak. But the warmth I felt behind the scenes, the genuine tears of many who took part in those morning entertainment broadcasts, were not due to professional duty.

"When we decided to organize a concert at the Rome Auditorium on Saturday, March 5, hoping that it would be a celebration of your liberation (subsequently cancelled because of the tragedy of Nicola's death), the willingness to participate on the part of every artist contacted was absolute, even at the price of some sacrifice. We met the same total cooperation in terms of offering us time on television shows or in theaters to tell your story or make appeals for your liberation.

"It remains to be seen how much of this mobilization, this involvement and willingness to commit to a cause, has survived. How much of this demand for a new political course is lying dormant, or has become part of the [strategy] of the center-left?

"Frankly, I believe none of it has, and I don't know why. I don't know where the responsibility lies: maybe a bit with us, or maybe it's simply that no one on the current political scene has the tools or the ability to take full advantage of these new developments. The power of the political demands represented by ordinary people who participated for the first time in a demonstration, or the emotions that lay behind those children's drawings, make us examine not only our relationships with political movements, which are often reduced to slogans or the imaginings of some presumed leader, but they also force us to rethink our interpretive categories. That's an undertaking that does not seem within reach of the leadership of the left, save for a few exceptions. But here we risk getting off the subject."

Getting back, seeing the photos, hearing the stories, I noticed that all your actions were marked by an optimism which must have stemmed both from the success of the demonstrations, and the ongoing negotiations. From inside my prison, I could sense that negotiations were under way as well, and this helped me to hope.

"Naturally, we knew little of the negotiations or contacts. We could only guess at the political nature [of the talks] and at the timeline, which proceeded fairly quickly and with tangible results. The proof [that they were holding you] arrived (the letter, etc.). This link [with your captors] was uninterrupted until the crisis provoked by another effort at mediation, that of Maurizio Scelli, the interim commissioner of the Italian Red Cross. His efforts—motivated, seemingly, only by personal ambition—probably delayed your liberation, as has been amply written about recently. This was a moment of real crisis—today, I can't help but wonder how things might have turned out had that intrusion never occurred.

"During this entire period, I had the opportunity (within limits, obviously) to get to know the work of the Italian intelligence agency, SISMI. Beyond their undeniable professionalism, they seemed to me to reach a new level of passion and commitment in dealing with your situation, above and beyond the call of duty, perhaps out of a real appreciation for your work."

One of them told me that they'd hung a photo of me on a blackboard in their office, and every night before leaving they would wish me goodnight, and tell me that I'd soon be free.

"This is where the relationship with Calipari begins. I got to know him only late in the game, after the arrival of your video. Until then, he'd had more contact with Gabriele."

Speaking of the video, what impression did it make on you? You've told me of the reaction of the general public, but what was your impression, and Calipari's, given that it was the reason for your first meeting?

"The first assessment—although this might seem paradoxical—was reassuring. Not just because it was concrete proof that you were alive, but also because your condition, beyond the drama of the situation, was comforting: you weren't bound, there were no signs of violence, you weren't veiled in black, there were no armed men, your hair was loose. Looking at it again and again, it was clear from the terminology used that you were following orders, reciting a script. Anyway, you seemed to have your wits about you, like you were able—even in that tragic situation—to handle your predicament. One thing we noticed was how the Italian and French versions corresponded, as though you had learned a prearranged part by memory. That impression was confirmed by the fact that at a certain point you interrupted yourself to say that you made a mistake, that you had to start again—you seemed somehow to be doing it intentionally. That aside, the crude and dramatic nature of the message affected me profoundly, particularly because you appealed to me personally … it was like a punch in the stomach. As it must have been for anyone seeing it who couldn't follow our reasoning.

"These impressions of mine were reinforced by Calipari, who instantly gave me the impression of being down-to-earth, serious, thoughtful, and determined. His words and arguments were decisive in convincing me that the road we were following was the right one, that SISMI's efforts were paying off and would obtain results. Let me be clear: he never made it seem like we could take a positive outcome for granted. He never told me everything would be OK. He just said: we're on the right track, we're working at it, there will be results, but always keep in mind that there are many pitfalls along the way."

Yet his attitude was conducive to maintaining a certain optimism.

"He gave the impression that everything possible was being done. The most critical period in these cases is right after the abduction, when you don't yet know whom you're dealing with and any little hitch could bring everything crashing down. Then the situation solidifies and you follow a path. That doesn't mean focusing on a single channel, but a methodical search for someone to deal with, someone willing to engage [in negotiations]. Our optimism was a byproduct of the concrete course they were following, which had yielded results in the past, and the nature of the abduction, which led us to exclude the worst hypotheses. Past experience—including the terrible fate of Baldoni [Enzo Baldoni, an Italian reporter executed in 2004 by kidnappers who called themselves the Islamic Army]—also seemed to indicate that once you got over a certain period, given the nature of the abduction, there was no longer any benefit in killing the hostage; that is, naturally, if negotiations were under way."

What did you think of the claims of responsibility or announcements of my execution...

"Those announcements were preceded by information from SISMI that indicated they were unfounded—although they certainly had an effect on us anyway. But they were regularly followed up by denials."

Were you all expecting my liberation?

"Yes, that Friday I thought I would be leaving for the Gulf to come and get you. Actually, I had thought that before—at the beginning of the week, Calipari had left to conclude the negotiations and everything seemed like the time was growing near. So, on Friday, when the news [of your liberation] was first announced by Al Jazeera, it didn't surprise me. Then the telephone went crazy and I headed in to *Il Manifesto*. From there, Gabriele and I ran over to Palazzo Chigi, followed by a few journalists. We entered through the back door, without even a security check, and went up to Gianni Letta's office, where we also found SISMI director Nicolo Pollari, and one of his agents.

"Then Berlusconi comes in. Pollari had already spoken with you, and he steps out of the room to try and call again so I can speak to you as well. Instead, he comes back in, all agitated, and tells us what is happening—he has the driver on the line talking about 300 or 400 shots fired at the car. Faced with our incredulity, he asks the driver again. He immediately relays the news that Nicola is dead. And the woman? First the driver says he can see you, that you have your eyes open, that you're moving, and then you stand up … During those minutes we can only guess what has happened we know nothing for sure. Nicola is dead, this seems certain, although we all hope he's just unconscious from his wounds. And your condition is unclear as well.

"At this point, a terrible thing happens: the agent says he has a rifle pointed at his ear and he has to turn off the cell phone. The SISMI director is urging him to tell the soldiers that he's on the line with the Italian government, but the agent makes clear that the American soldiers don't care what he says, and the call breaks off. This is followed by fifteen discouraging minutes of gloom and impotence. That's the exact sensation: an impotence beyond words, in the face of such arrogance, of an American ally that makes its own decisions and does whatever it wants—although, frankly, even I didn't think they'd go this far. We're only a subordinate ally, at times inconvenient, never able to operate as an equal. What to do? Who to call? How to reestablish communication? Berlusconi is silent—maybe he's already foreseeing the explosive effects that will follow. Letta is trying to find Minister [of Defense] Antonio Martino; the Italian ambassador in Baghdad, Gianludovico De Martino; and the American ambassador. Another SISMI agent arrives, and speaks to Pollari: they decide to leave for Baghdad. Berlusconi tells them to take me with them. At that point, we organize the departure to come get you, even though we don't yet know if you can be moved. Gabriele heads back to the paper. I stay for a few more minutes. I'm uneasy about something: I ask Berlusconi what will be said about everything that's just happened. Because at that moment, I didn't know that Nicola's death would become an element of national pride—although now, thinking it over, it seems like it was inevitable. But it isn't just a matter of Nicola's death: there is a secret operation under way, conducted by Italian agents who have been fired on by the Americans. Others may be involved or in danger. I ask what version of events will be given out. As I leave Palazzo Chigi, what can I say to those who will ask me what happened? Berlusconi doesn't hesitate: "The whole truth," he responds dryly. I leave. I stop at home to gather some things for you, though I have no idea what might be useful. I grab a jacket, in any case. I leave for Ciampino Airport, in a SISMI car, which like any other, has to stop off to get gas. After a breathless search for the telephone number of Palazzo Chigi—I didn't bring it with me, and the agent accompanying me doesn't have it either—I manage to talk to Letta, who in the meantime has been able to get in touch with you. This reassures me. When we get to Ciampino, the SISMI agent organizing our trip is on the phone with the American military personnel in control of Baghdad Airport.

They don't want to let us land before six in the morning, when it's light. The agent refuses to be intimidated: we're taking off anyway, we have the authorization of the Italian prime minister; if you don't want to let us land, shoot us down. At that point, it's already eleven o'clock, and we're ready to leave—a full-fledged team has formed, with around ten people, including a doctor. We get to Baghdad in about three and a half hours. It's four thirty, Baghdad time. There is some problem about finding the two helicopters to take us to the hospital where they are treating you. But in the end, we find them, and we make it to the hospital. You know the story from there."

ELEVEN

CONCLUSIONS

IT HAPPENED maybe twice, that both my guards went out, leaving me alone in the apartment/prison where I was being held hostage. When I'd knock on the door and no one would respond or come to open it, I would be assailed by a sudden fear of abandonment, adding to the anguish provoked by my unbearable claustrophobia. The thought that I might die locked in my room, like a bird in a cage, or worse, like a mouse in a trap, terrified me. Even today, when I think back on those moments, I relive the terror, and I'm seized by the fear of abandonment, by an anxiety I can do nothing to control.

It's not the only legacy of my imprisonment. In the midst of my captivity, forced to pass my days alone without being able to exchange a word or thought with another person, I dreamed of losing myself in the crowd—not just to talk, but to listen to the voices. Now, when I find myself in a large group of people, I'm seized by anxiety instead. Crowds scare me. On the streets, I can't escape from people who recognize me, mostly women. They often stop me, discreetly, and say: "We're proud of you, keep at it." Embarrassed, I ask myself why. Sometimes I feel the need to be alone—which friends don't understand—to face up to myself and to my numerous fears. Like fear of the dark: I can't fall asleep anymore with the lights off. At times I wake up in a sudden panic: where am I? The light reassures me of my surroundings.

A sense of insecurity has remained with me in everything I do, from crossing the street to driving a car. It's probably this insecurity that keeps me living day-to-day, fearful of making plans for the future. Although, more than my captivity, I think it's the effect of what happened after my liberation: the shooting shattered an emotion I was just beginning to feel, the joy of being set free. This emotion was brutally shattered; I can never be happy about my liberation, because it cost the life of the person who saved me.

Still, thanks to Nicola Calipari, I am alive and free. And maybe, little by little, I'll be able to conquer my fears and my anguish, to regain trust in myself and make plans for the future. Before this tragic adventure, I no sooner returned from one trip than I began planning another. Now this restlessness seems trapped inside me. Perhaps I'll recapture my former self: certainly I will never stop fighting, starting now, to know the truth about the death of Nicola Calipari.

My abduction had a dual effect: frustration on the professional level and confirmation on the political level. Until the eve of my last departure for Baghdad, I maintained that despite the danger of the situation, it was necessary to run the risks and inform the public about the devastating effects of the war in Iraq. Some of us were willing to run those risks. But now I'm forced to admit that it's no longer possible to work in Iraq today; to do the job as I believe it should be done, getting out in the streets, reporting on the daily effects of the war, witnessing the suffering, speaking with the protagonists of the Iraqi reality. I went to interview the refugees from Falluja, among those who have suffered most under the occupation, and I was kidnapped. To be abducted while interviewing refugees, perhaps precisely because you are interviewing refugees, is the demonstration that in Iraq, the armed don't want any witnesses. To have to accept this imposition is in some way a defeat. Not only for me, but for all those in Iraq who need to make their voices heard. I tried to give a voice to the voiceless in every area of conflict—from Somalia to Algeria, from Palestine to Afghanistan, and until my abduction, in Iraq as well. Evidently—and this is my one regret—I had not calculated how far the degeneration of war could reach. It was my abductors who shoved that cold, hard reality in my face. In Iraq, all the possible parameters for safeguarding oneself are gone; it's like finding yourself in a swamp, not knowing where to put your feet. Not that I believed myself immune to the danger of abduction. On the contrary: I always kept the bare minimum for survival in captivity in my purse. But my abduction forced me to admit that it no longer made sense to risk so much in order to report. The abduction was the proof that the armed resistance (or at least some of its factions) is not interested in having a relationship with the outside world, given that it treats all foreigners as enemies. It no longer makes any distinction between the soldiers occupying the country, contractors waging a dirty war, humanitarian workers working side by side with the most needy, and journalists who want to report on a different reality than that seen by embedded reporters through the filter (or censor) of military command. Today, because of my abduction, I'm forced to say that I will not return to Iraq until the situation changes—and that's an admission of defeat.

What happened to me after my liberation, the car hit by "friendly fire," took me back to the real origins of the current situation in Iraq: the war. The violent fall of Saddam did not bring liberty, but the decline into barbarism of Mesopotamia, cradle of civilization of the Sumerians, the Assyrians, and the Babylonians. This is the reality.

For anyone with the patience to read to the end of this book, the dual sense of the title should be clear.

"Friendly fire" refers not only to the shots fired by American soldiers at the car in which I was riding—shots that killed Nicola Calipari—but also to those "fired" at me by my abductors. I had always fought against the war and the occupation of Iraq, yet I was kidnapped by those who said they were fighting for the liberation of their own country. What's more, I was abducted while I searched for witnesses to the effects of the bombs that destroyed Falluja, while I tried to give a voice to those who could not speak through embedded journalists. Why me, specifically? It's the question that tormented me during my captivity—which, thankfully, is over. And then, the anguished question: why Nicola Calipari? Will we ever have an answer? We cannot give up on the search for the truth.

APPENDIXES

APPENDIX A

SGRENA SETS THE RECORD STRAIGHT: "THERE WAS NO CHECKPOINT; NO SELF-DEFENSE"

By Jeremy Scahill
Published on www.counterpunch.org
March 28, 2005

Giuliana Sgrena would probably be the first to say that to focus on her case would be to miss the point of the extent of the daily, horrific violence Iraqis face at the hands of U.S. soldiers. Sgrena is the Italian war correspondent who was shot by U.S. forces as she was en route to the Baghdad airport after being freed from a month of being held hostage by an Iraqi resistance group. She knows better than most that if she and the senior Italian intelligence official killed by U.S. troops as he tried to save her were merely Iraqi civilians, this would be even more of a non-story than it already is in the U.S. press.

With Terri Schiavo and Michael Jackson to cover, it is pretty difficult for most media outlets to find the time to report on any of the more than 100,000 Iraqi civilians killed since the beginning of the invasion two years ago. That's why cases like Sgrena's become so important—because they represent a chance to show the world part of the reality Iraqis face every day of their lives: they are kidnapped in alarming numbers; they are shot by trigger-happy U.S. soldiers; their deaths are justified—if they are even acknowledged—by U.S. officials floating flimsy cover stories that would never stand up in any U.S. court (except perhaps a military court).

©2005 Jeremy Scahill. Reprinted with permission.

New details are emerging about Sgrena's shooting and the death of the Italian official, Nicola Calipari, that bear reporting in English (this, of course, remains a significant story in Italy). Independent journalist Naomi Klein recently met with Sgrena in the Rome military hospital where she has been since returning to Italy on March 5.

"Giuliana is quite a bit sicker than we have been led to believe," says Klein. "She was fired on by a gun at the top of a tank, which means that the artillery was very, very large. It was a four-inch bullet that entered her body and broke apart. And it didn't just injure her shoulder, it punctured her lung. Her lung continues to fill with fluid and there continue to be complications stemming from that fairly serious injury."

This case has been written off by U.S. officials as a "horrific accident" that occurred on what we are told is "the most dangerous road in Iraq," where insurgents are constantly waiting in the bushes to attack. The Pentagon further contends that the Italians failed to slow down at a checkpoint and only after repeated attempts to stop the car did soldiers fire on the Italians.

Klein says that Sgrena is very frustrated by the U.S. government's claim, repeated consistently by the media, that the Italians were fired at from a checkpoint. "She says it wasn't a checkpoint at all," Klein says. "It was simply a tank parked on the side of the road that opened fire on them. There was no process of trying to stop the car, she said, or any signals. From her perspective, it was just a tank opening fire."

"It was not a checkpoint. Nobody asked us to stop," Sgrena told Klein "They didn't try to stop us, they just shot us. They have a way to signal us to stop but they didn't give us any signals to stop and they were at least ten meters off the street to the side."

Sgrena also says that the U.S. soldiers fired at them from behind, which of course contradicts the claim that the soldiers fired in self-defense. "Part of what we're hearing is that the U.S. soldiers opened fire on their car, because they didn't know who they were, and they were afraid," says Klein. "The fear, of course, is that their car could have blown up or that the soldiers might come under attack themselves. And what Giuliana Sgrena really stressed with me was that the bullet that injured her so badly came from behind, entered through the back of the car. And the only person who was not severely injured in the car was the driver, and she said that this is because the shots weren't coming from the front."

"They were coming from the right and behind, i.e., they were driving away. So, the idea that this was an act of self-defense, I think becomes much more questionable," says Klein. "Because if indeed the majority of the gunfire is coming from behind, then clearly, the soldiers were firing at a car that was driving away from them."

That could explain why the U.S. military in Iraq has blocked the Italian government from inspecting the Italians' vehicle, even though the car is the property of the Italian government, which bought it from the rental agency after this incident. "I think they have something to hide if they won't give the car over for inspection," Sgrena told Klein. "It's very strange. If there is nothing to hide, why not let Italian justice officials see the car?"

"It was not self-defense," Sgrena said. "The soldiers were to the right of us on the side of the road, they started to shoot from the right and kept shooting from behind but most of the shots came from behind, Calipari was shot from the right and I was shot in the shoulder from behind. When we stopped, they were behind us. We could see that all the back windows of the car were broken from behind. If they are afraid, they can stop the car, they can ask it to stop, then you can shoot at the wheels but they didn't do that. They didn't try to stop the car and they shot at least ten bullets at the level of people sitting inside the car. If Calipari had not pushed me down, they could have killed me."

This case sheds important light on the culture of impunity surrounding the U.S. occupation of Iraq. If this is how Washington treats Italy, one of its closest allies in the so-called war on terror, when U.S. soldiers kill the country's second-highest ranking intelligence official, imagine the struggle Iraqis face as they die in the tens of thousands. They don't have a powerful figure like Sylvio Berlusconi to advocate for them. Instead, they have unembedded reporters like Giuliana Sgrena who risk their lives to tell these stories.

"You have to protect the life of journalists who are going and speaking to the people," says Luciana Castellina, one of the founders of Sgrena's newspaper *Il Manifesto*. "Otherwise, the result would be that we wouldn't have any journalists anymore or only the embedded journalists."

APPENDIX B

GIULIANA SGRENA BLASTS U.S. COVER-UP, CALLS FOR U.S. AND ITALY TO LEAVE IRAQ

DEMOCRACY NOW! INTERVIEW WITH
AMY GOODMAN AND JUAN GONZALEZ
APRIL 27, 2005

AMY GOODMAN: In her most extended interview to date in the U.S., Italian journalist Giuliana Sgrena blasts a Pentagon report that clears the U.S. soldiers who opened fire on her car, wounding her and killing one of Italy's highest-ranking intelligence officials. Sgrena says, "It is important that the Americans press their government to tell the truth. Because it is in the interest of Americans, the truth. Not only of Italians."

We begin today with the ongoing controversy over the killing of one of Italy's highest-ranking intelligence officials by U.S. soldiers last month in Baghdad. On Monday, a U.S. Army official reported that a military investigation has cleared the soldiers who shot dead Nicola Calipari on March 4 after U.S. troops opened fire on the car that was also carrying Giuliana Sgrena—the Italian journalist who had just been freed from captivity. Sgrena has publicly rejected the U.S. claims that the shooting was justified. The leaking of that report sparked outrage in Italy.

The Italian officials on the U.S.-led commission are reportedly refusing to endorse the U.S. Army's findings. Italy maintains that that car carrying Calipari and Sgrena had been driving slowly, received no warning, and that Italy had advised U.S. authorities of their mission to evacuate Sgrena from Iraq.

Italian judges are conducting a separate investigation into the killing. The report comes at a bad time for Italian Prime Minister Silvio Berlusconi, who was forced to resign last week in the wake of his center-right coalition's defeat in recent regional elections. The defeat was blamed in large part on Berlusconi's unpopular decision to send troops to Iraq. He quickly put together a new cabinet, hoping to cling to power through elections due next spring.

Yesterday, Giuliana Sgrena blasted the results of the investigation at a news conference in Rome:

> I didn't have great confidence in this inquiry given the past experiences of similar incidents and inquiries. Obviously, if what leaked today was the result of the inquiry, then it's even worse than what I had anticipated, because earlier the Americans had spoken about a tragic mistake and they had somehow taken on some responsibilities. Now they seem unwilling to accept responsibility.

The U.S. government has said it will not comment on the report until it is officially released. This is Secretary of State Donald Rumsfeld and Chairman of the Joint Chiefs of Staff Richard Myers, speaking at a news conference at the Pentagon yesterday:

> DONALD RUMSFELD: My latest information is that they have not come to a final agreement on a joint report, and the—it will—whatever is issued will be issued in the period ahead and we'll know when it's issued. It's an investigation. It was done together intimately, and I think that we'll just have to wait and see what they come out with.

> RICHARD MYERS: I would say it will most likely be announced in Baghdad. That's the plan right now, when they come to their final conclusions.

REPORTER: Has the report essentially found that American troops will not be punished in this—

RICHARD MYERS: It's not final yet, so we cannot say.

REPORTER: So it hasn't determined whether or not—

RICHARD MYERS: We haven't seen the report. General Casey, he's still got the report.

REPORTER: Is there the possibility it that it might be two separate reports?

RICHARD MYERS: Don't know. We'll have to wait and see, and it will be announced in Baghdad.

Yesterday, I spoke with Giuliana Sgrena by telephone from Rome, where she is recovering from the injuries she suffered as a result of the shooting. I began by asking her reaction to the Pentagon report.

SGRENA: Yes, for the moment we have not seen an official result of the reports, but we have some rumors about the conclusion of the report, so I am very sad about that because I was—it was words that I was waiting for. I thought that maybe the Americans would speak of an accident or something like that, but now they say that the U.S. military has no responsibility for what happened on the fourth of March in Baghdad. They say that they respected all the engagement rules, and that is not true, because I was there and I can testify that they just shot at us without any advertising [warning], any intention, any attempt to stop us before that. So I think that it's very bad, this conclusion, because they don't want to assume any responsibility, and they don't care that our testimony—mine and that of the Italian intelligence agent—that these were quite the same. We were there and we are in a position to testify about what happened, so it's not true what the Americans say, what the commission says. So we are very afraid, we are very worried about that. Also the Italian government, for the moment, doesn't accept this conclusion, nor do the Italian members that were in the commission, so it is a very bad situation. They wanted to give a strike to the Italian government even if they are allies in the war in Iraq.

GOODMAN: Giuliana, the U.S. military says your car was going very fast.

SGRENA: That's not true, because we were slow, and we were slowing down, because we had to turn. Before the turn, there was some water, so it's not true that the car was going fast.

GOODMAN: They say the soldiers used hand and arm signals, flashed white lights, and fired warning shots to get the driver to stop.

SGRENA: No, they didn't. No, no. No light, no air fire, nothing at all. They were beside the road. They were not on the street. They were ten meters away, and they didn't give us any sign that they were there, so we didn't see them before they started to shoot.

GOODMAN: Did they shoot from the front or from the back?

SGRENA: No, from the back, not from the front. They shot from the back, because Calipari was in the back on the right and he was shot dead immediately, and I was injured on my shoulder, but I was shot from the back. So I am proof that they were shooting from the back and not from the front of the car. We can see by my injury where I was shot.

GOODMAN: Did the Italians do this report with the U.S. military?

SGRENA: There were two Italians on the commission, but they don't accept the conclusions of the commission, so now there is some discussion between the Italian authorities and the American ambassador here in Rome. But the two members of the commission, they don't accept the conclusion of the commission, so there is a problem.

GOODMAN: Were the Italians able to inspect the car?

SGRENA: No, we were expecting the car tonight in Rome, so that the judges who are doing the normal inquiry could see the car. I hope to see the car also, but we don't know what the condition of the car will be like. And the Italian judges, they also don't know the names of the soldiers that were involved in the shooting.

GOODMAN: The other person in the car.

SGRENA: Yes.

GOODMAN: Did the two of you testify?

SGRENA: Yes, he gave the same testimony as me, but the Americans, the commission, didn't take into account our testimony. It seems to be like that, because they didn't mention our testimony.

GOODMAN: After they shot you and killed Calipari, what happened to the other man?

SGRENA: The other man got out of the car and was shouting that we were Italian and from the embassy, and he was speaking on the telephone with the Italian government. And we have, my husband, for example, he was there listening to the call. And at a certain moment the soldiers, they imposed to these agents, because these were Italian intelligence agents, and they imposed him to cut the call with weapons.

GOODMAN: Say that again. What did they do?

SGRENA: They stopped him from—he was talking by telephone with an Italian member of the government. Berlusconi was there with his advisor, Letta, plus the chief of intelligence, my husband, and the director of my newspaper, because they were there waiting for news of our liberation. And they were talking about the shooting and at a certain moment, an American soldier stopped him and with a weapon forced him to cut the communication.

GOODMAN: And then what happened?

SGRENA: And then what happened I don't know, because I was injured, so they brought me to the hospital, and I don't know what happened to the other man, to the other agent.

GOODMAN: Did you get permission, did Calipari get permission, to drive on the road to the airport?

SGRENA: Of course, I was there when they called. They called an Italian, because there is an official that is linked to the Americans. And this Italian general spoke to Captain Green, an American, telling him that we were on this road and to make sure they were aware that we were on that road. And this happened at least twenty to twenty-five minutes before the shooting.

GOODMAN: This road…

SGRENA: They knew that we were on this road.

GOODMAN: How do you know that they knew?

SGRENA: I know because I was there when the agent called the Italian general that is in charge of communication with the Americans. And this general testified, saying that he was there with Captain Green, and Captain Green was immediately informed about our traveling to the airport. And Captain Green didn't deny that, so I think that the Italian general is right. And he's a general. I don't think that this general gave a wrong or false testimony.

GOODMAN: So you're saying Calipari spoke to—this was an Italian or U.S. general?

SGRENA: The Italians, they can't speak to the Americans directly. There is a man, a special man, a general that is in charge of communication with the American commanders. It's impossible for an agent, an Italian agent, to speak with the Americans directly. I know the rules because I was there many times. And I know that every time always in Iraq there is an Italian that is in charge of communication with the Americans. And this time, in this moment, there was a general that was speaking with Captain Green, who was the correspondent, the American one. So I knew about that. And that was published in all the newspapers, Italian newspapers. So there was no problem of communication. Captain Green knew about our presence on that road. We don't know if he didn't inform the mobile patrol. But he knew, the American commander knew about it.

GOODMAN: And where did the conversation take place? Was it in the Green Zone?

SGRENA: I don't know. I don't know. I didn't follow the general, because many officials are in places in the Green Zone that I don't know. I can't know where the generals are. It's a secret place. Because it is very dangerous in Baghdad, they don't say where they meet.

GOODMAN: Giuliana, can you explain the road? This wasn't the regular Baghdad—the road to the airport that you traveled on? This was a special road?

SGRENA: Yes. It was a special road for people that are working in embassies, or they are Americans, or they are contractors. Special people that go to the airport.

GOODMAN: And did Calipari inform the Americans when he arrived in Iraq what he was doing?

SGRENA: I don't know. This I don't know. I can't testify about it. But I think that the intelligence has the possibility to do—anyway, he got a badge from the U.S. commanders, because he had to go around with weapons and such. But I don't know what he told the Americans he wanted to do. I can't say.

GOODMAN: You mean a badge he got, like permission to go?

SGRENA: Yes. I don't know. To move around in Iraq you need a badge. And Calipari got a badge from the American commanders in the airport. And they knew that he was there with a car, with weapons, and with another agent, and all these kinds of things, because if not, he couldn't go around. But what he really said to the Americans, I can't say. I can't know. They are intelligence. They don't say to other people like me what they say, what they are doing. You know?

GOODMAN: Giuliana, did you encounter any other U.S. military on that road before you were shot?

SGRENA: No, we didn't.

GOODMAN: And where did Calipari pick you up? How did you get rescued?

SGRENA: I don't know, but I was not—I was covered.

GOODMAN: Right now, do you think that Prime Minister Silvio Berlusconi is doing enough in your case?

SGRENA: Yes, because I am free. I think that he did enough before. Now I don't know what he is doing. But before, he did, because I am free now, you know? And I am happy to be free.

GOODMAN: What do think should happen right now?

SGRENA: I don't know.

GOODMAN: What are you calling for?

SGRENA: I am calling for the withdrawal of the troops.

GOODMAN: From Iraq?

SGRENA: Yes, of course. The Italian troops from Iraq, and also the Americans. But for the moment, as I am Italian, I ask for the withdrawal of the Italian ones. But my desire would be the withdrawal of all troops from Iraq.

GOODMAN: Are you satisfied that Berlusconi has said they will pull out the troops by the end of the year?

SGRENA: I am not so sure they will, so before, I want to wait to see if they will really withdraw all the troops.

GOODMAN: And in terms of your report right now, the U.S. military is saying the Italians don't want to sign off on it. Will the Italian commissioners sign this report?

SGRENA: I don't know. How can I know? I can't meet the Italian members.

GOODMAN: Do you feel like a fair investigation has been done?

SGRENA: No, I don't think so.

GOODMAN: Who do you think should be held responsible?

SGRENA: I don't know. I wanted to know, but if there are no further inquiries, it's impossible to know.

GOODMAN: Right now, you are calling for the troops to come out. Are you now continuing to write about Iraq? How are you feeling?

SGRENA: Now I am very bad, because my physical situation is very bad, so I can't work for the moment. This is my problem. I am not well, I am very sick. I am going every day to the hospital. I am very tired, you know?

GOODMAN: Where did the bullet lodge in your body?

SGRENA: The bullet was in the shoulder, but some pieces reached the lung, so I am very, very sick.

GOODMAN: And your time in captivity, do you know who held you? And how were you treated?

SGRENA: I was treated normally, from the material point of view. But I was a prisoner, so I was without freedom. And this was very terrible. But I didn't know where I was. I was in Baghdad, but I don't know where.

GOODMAN: And do you know who held you?

SGRENA: No.

GOODMAN: We all saw the videotape. What were the circumstances of the videotape?

SGRENA: Of course when you are a hostage, they tell you what you have to do, what you have to say, you know? But I don't like so much to speak about my period of kidnapping, because I already spoke so much about it that every time that I think about it I am so sick. That is bad for my health, you know? I always go back to these things and I prefer it, if possible, not to speak so much about that, because it is very bad for my health.

GOODMAN: President Bush. Do you have a demand of the U.S. president?

SGRENA: No. I want only the truth. But they don't seem to be interested in finding the truth about what happened in Baghdad that night.

GOODMAN: Will you go back to Iraq?

SGRENA: No.

GOODMAN: What will you do?

SGRENA: I don't know. For the moment, I don't know. I have to take care of my health, you know? I am very bad—in a very bad situation.

GOODMAN: Do you feel like there is a cover-up here?

SGRENA: Yes, of course. They don't want the truth. They don't want to tell the truth.

GOODMAN: What would make them tell the truth?

SGRENA: I don't know. I don't know. I don't really know. Maybe if the

Americans, if they press the American government to tell the truth. Because we are small, we are Italians, we are few Italians—what can we do? I think that it is important that the Americans, they press their government to tell the truth, because it's in the interest also of Americans, the truth. Not only of Italians, I think. So if you take action to press on the government, you, maybe you can do something for us.

GOODMAN: And when you were in Iraq, as a reporter, before you were captured, what do you think was the most important story for us all to understand?

SGRENA: I was looking around to see what the people were thinking about. And overall, I was interested in Falluja. But when I went to interview some people from Falluja, I was kidnapped. Some people were not interested in my story about Falluja, I think.

GOODMAN: What did you have to say about Falluja? What did you discover?

SGRENA: Just stories. I don't have a scoop about Falluja, just stories.

GOODMAN: Why did you go to Iraq to begin with? It was a dangerous place. You knew that.

SGRENA: Yes, I knew. But I am a journalist. I went to Somalia. I went to Afghanistan. I went to Algeria. I went everywhere. And I went to Iraq also. I can't go only where it's not dangerous. It is our work that is dangerous.

GOODMAN: Do you regret having gone to Iraq?

SGRENA: No, I don't.

GOODMAN: And in the car, before you were shot and Calipari was killed, what did he say to you? What did you talk about?

SGRENA: About the liberation, about experiences. About I don't remember, really. I was very happy to be free. But I was happy only for twenty minutes, and then it was finished. And now I am very sad. I am in a lot of pain, I am very tired.

GOODMAN: Well, I want to thank you very much for being with us.

SGRENA: Thank you.

INDEX

Abadan, port of, 152
Abdallah, 21, 23
Abu Ghraib, 66, 69, 104, 121–22
Adhamiya, 94, 137
Afghan, 38, 98–99, 131
Afghanistan, 10, 34, 38, 43, 53, 92, 96, 98, 106, 118, 131, 170, 187, 206
Africa, 54
Algeria, 10, 43, 53, 68, 83, 108, 117, 187, 206
Ali, 101, 112
Allawi, Ali, 147
Allawi, Iyad, 31, 130, 143
Alwani, Abdul Jabbar Kadhim al, 35
Alwash, Azzam, 76
Alwash, Suzie, 77
American Civil Liberties Union, 127
Amman, 33, 74
ANSA, 37, 169
Arab, 19, 34, 45, 53, 57, 67, 84, 91–93, 107–109, 115, 117, 129, 138, 141–42, 149, 171
Arabic, 25–26, 54, 67–68, 103, 108, 119, 166, 176
Al Arabiya, 66
ARCI (Italian Association of Recreation and Culture), 52
Army Corps of Engineers, 98
Ashura, 101
Assyrians, 142, 187

Aubenas, Florence, 29, 68, 86–87
Australia, 10, 115
Baath Party, 33, 89–91, 108, 127, 144, 146, 148–49, 171
Babylonians, 187
Badr Brigades, 148, 150, 151
Badrani, Fadhil, 26
Baghdad Institute of Forensic Medicine, 122
Bahily, Hamid al, 80
Bakr, Faeq Ameen, 122
Balad, 90
Baldoni, Enzo, 48, 180
Balkan War, 52, 78
Baquba, 90, 139
Baradei, Mohammed el, 79
Barzani, 52
Basra, 48, 70, 77, 130–31, 135, 145, 148–49, 152
Basri, Assad al, 130
Bayati, Salman Dawood al, 134
BBC, 97
Beirut, 153
Benetollo, Tom, 52
Bennis, Phyllis, 80
Berlusconi, Silvio, 49–50, 55, 84–85, 88, 175–76, 181–83, 194, 196, 200, 203, 210–11
The Betrothed of Allah, 108

Biladati, 70
bin Laden, Osama, 96, 136
black market, 21, 40, 45, 73
Blackwater, 33
Blair, Tony, 50, 172
Bloom, David, 8
Bremer, L. Paul, 33
British, 50, 70, 71, 80, 97, 98, 127, 149, 150
the Bureau of Immigration, 161
burka, 59, 96, 117, 121
Bush, George W., 14, 70, 89, 97, 99, 109, 113, 139, 146, 153, 163, 166, 172, 175, 205, 210

Calipari, Nicola, 9, 13, 61, 155–57, 161–62, 166, 177–79, 181–82, 186, 188, 192–95, 198–202, 207, 209–10
Calipari, Rosa, 161, 167
Camp Baharia, 32
Camp Victory, 38, 164
Campidoglio, 87, 173
Campregher, Pierluigi, 163
Canada, 76
Captain Drew, 164, 165
Captain Green, 165, 200, 201
Carpani, Andrea, 156, 158, 162, 163, 166
Carraro, Franco, 173
Casey, George, 197
Castellina, Luciana, 194
Castro, Fidel, 104
Celio military hospital, 161
Cermis, 167
Cessna, 52
Chaldeans, 114, 142
Chechnya, 108
checkpoint, 24, 31, 34, 45, 62, 163, 165, 191, 192, 209
Cheney, Dick, 73
Cholera, 21, 53
Christian Science Monitor, 90
Christians, 104, 105, 114, 115, 130, 145
CIA, 130
Ciampi, Carlo Azeglio, 162, 211
Ciampino Airport, 182, 209

Coalition Provisional Authority, 126
Comiso, 51
Commission for Compensation of Falluja Citizens, 31
Communist Party, Iraq, 138, 152
Communist Party, Italy, 211
conscientious objectors, 13

Danube, 78
Davud, Juliana Youssef, 131
Dawa, 110, 113, 143, 152
Democracy Now!, 10, 195
Democratic Party, 140
Dhari, Hareth al, 95, 144, 153
Die Zeit, 28
Diliberto, Oliviero, 211
al Dora, 73, 78
Dossier on Civilian Casualties in Iraq 2003–2005, 70
Dulaimi, Adnan al, 150
Dulaimi, Hafid al, 31
Dulaimi, Saadoun al, 152

Eden Again Project, 76, 77
Egyptian, 135, 148
El Diario, 27
elections, Iraq, Jan 2005, 19, 31, 40, 96, 112, 129, 130, 134, 136, 139–40, 142–45, 172, 196
electricity, 22, 40, 41, 72, 73, 98
English, 4, 11, 12, 26, 58, 68, 86, 87, 103, 119, 131, 166, 192
Erbil, 97, 141, 147
EuroNews, 49, 87

Fadel, Leila, 75
Falangist, 153
Falluja, 9, 17–27, 29, 30–35, 66–67, 70, 72, 90, 96, 98, 114, 137, 139, 148, 186, 188, 206
Falujan refugees, 9, 17, 19–21, 24–27, 29, 66, 105, 139, 186
fatwa, 24, 110, 112, 143
Fawzia, 24, 121
Fayyad, Haifa, 75

fedayeen, 53, 92
Federcalcio, 173
Fini, Gianfranco, 162, 171, 210
Finland, 78
fundamentalism, 96, 102, 108, 151

Garabet, Celia, 130
gas, 21, 22, 40, 45, 73, 74, 144, 182
General Hospital, 17
Geneva, 72
Geneva Conventions, 71, 151
Graduate Institute of International Studies, 71
Greeks, 51
Green Zone, 113, 126, 127, 158, 201
Guantánamo, 69, 104
Guardian, 97, 127, 147
guerrillas, 35, 72, 90, 145, 148, †218
Gulf War I, 21, 48, 53, 76, 77, 79, 108, 131, 138

Haavisto, Pekka, 78
Hadeed, Mohammed, 27, 31
Haditha, 97, 98
Hakim, Abdelaziz al, 129, 143, 151, 152
Halabja, 96, 141
Haliburton, 73
Hamza, Khadar al Abbas, 79
Handra al Mohammadiya Mosque, 34
Hanifa, Abu, 93
Hanoun, Hussein, 87
Haqlania Bridge, 97
Haqqari, 53
Harlow, 126
Hashin, Mehdi Sabeen, 35
Hassan, Margaret, 50
Hawza, 110, 111, 112
Hejira, 101
Hilla, 69, 70
hittistes, 117
Holt, Lester, 8
Hotel Intercontinental, 117
Hotel Palestine, 53, 65
Hulago, 89
Human Rights Watch, 70

Hurricane Katrina, 80
Hussein, Saddam, 14, 25, 27, 33–34, 45–46, 53, 76, 89–90, 92–94, 96–97, 101, 104, 108–110, 113, 115, 121–22, 124, 128–29, 131, 133–36, 138, 140–41, 145–46, 148–49, 151–53, 164, 187
Hussein, Uday, 92

Il Manifesto, 43, 55, 104, 108, 155, 169, 170, 174, 176, 181, 194, 209
Infantry Battalion Tactical Operation Center, 164
Institute for Policy Studies and Foreign Policy, 80
International Atomic Energy Agency, 79, 80
Intisar, 127
Iran, 48, 53, 73, 77, 96, 101, 113–114, 117, 131, 138, 143, 151–53
Iranian Revolutionary Guards, 151
Iraq Body Count, 70, 71, 72
Iraq Today, 90
Iraqi police, 59, 60, 62, 63, 65, 93, 111, 148, 149, 150
Iraqi troops, 35, 149, 152
Al Iraqya, 66
Iraqya TV, 37, 49, 169
Islam, Islamic, 22, 24, 33, 34, 35, 53, 68, 85, 90–91, 94, 96–97, 102, 104, 106, 107, 108, 110, 111, 113–14, 121–24, 128–30, 141, 143, 148, 152, 180
Islamic Army, 180
Islamic Vendetta, 148
Italian Embassy, 30, 156, 199

Jaafari, Ibrahim al, 143, 150
Jabr, Bayan, 150
Jackson, Michael, 191
Jaish al Mahdi, 112, 136, 148
Japan, 76
Jawad, Hadil, 124, 125, 126
Al Jazeera, 66, 67, 86, 181
Jazim, Thair Ismael, 80
Jihad, 15, 49–50, 74, 88, 91–92, 114, 146

al Jihad, 75
Jihadists, 49–50, 91, 93
Jordan, 25, 30, 115
Juventus, 56

Al Kabir Mosque, 25
Kabul, 99, 106, 117–18, 131, 151
Kadhimiya, 137
Kadhimiya Mosque, 137, 153
Kalashnikovs, 44, 57, 68, 109, 130
Karbala, 48, 70, 92, 101–102, 107, 113
Khadim, Musa al, 137
Khadimya, 74
Khaled, Waleed, 66
Khalilzad, Zalmay, 99, 150
Khoi, Abd al, 112
Khomeini, Ayatollah, 113
al Kindi, 111
Kirkuk, 48, 125, 141–42, 144
Klein, Naomi, 192–93
Knight Ridder News Service, 75
Koran, 44, 56–57, 102, 105, 109, 129, 145
Koranic, 23–25, 33, 102
Krekar, Mullah, 96, 97
Kufa, 112
Kurdish Parliament, 153
Kurdish refugees, 53
Kurds, Kurdistan, 21, 52–53, 96, 97, 121, 124, 130, 134–35, 137–44, 146–47, 150, 153
Kut, 110
Kuwait, 73

L'Unità, 167
The Lancet, 71
Lash, Jonathan, 77
Latif, Mohammed, 33
Latin America, 54
Le Figaro, 130
Le Monde Diplomatique, 153
League of Iraqi Women, 121
Lebanese, 153
Letta, Gianni, 158, 170, 176, 181–82, 200
Libération, 29

Liqa, 126, 127
Lockerbie, 26
Lozano, Mario, 167

M-21, 90
madrassas, 23
Mahdi militia, 136
Al Majd TV, 95, 144, 153
Majid, 22, 23
Majlis, 152
Maki, Liqaa, 75, 76
Mandela, Nelson, 87
Manhaz, 87
Mansur, 74
marines, 18, 32, 34, 35, 92, 111, 145
Marioli, Mario, 165
Martino, Gianludovico de, 158, 182
Mashadani, Ali Omar Abraham al, 66
Mashhad, 113
Mazar i Sharif, 53
Measure 137, 129
Mediterranean Sea, 51
Mesopotamia, 29, 89, 115, 187
Milan, 43
military, Iraqi, 33, 35, 72, 78–79, 90, 92–93, 110, 121, 146–48, 152
military, U.S., 7, 9–10, 13–14, 27, 31–33, 38, 52, 62, 85, 112, 158, 162, 166, 182, 191, 193, 195, 197–98, 202, 203, 209
militia, 90, 97, 111, 112, 113, 136, 144, 147, 149
Miller, Geoffrey, 104
Mines Advisory Group, 78
Ministry of Defense, 27, 147
Minoui, 130, 131
Mithal, 121
Mogadishu, 52
Mohammed, Abu, 18
Mohammed, Yanar, 122
Mosul, 48, 97, 114, 139, 145, 148
Mount Cermis, 167
Al Mousawat, 125, 129
movimento pacifista, 12

Mualimchi, Amal al, 124
Muharram, 101
mujahideen, 33, 34, 44, 57, 83, 84, 86, 89, 90, 91, 94, 97, 98, 105, 117, 121
Mujahideen Without Borders, 84
mullahs, 110, 111, 113
Muslims, 28, 56, 58, 91, 92, 97, 105, 107, 108, 117, 129, 131
Mustafa Mosque, 20, 24, 28–29, 34
Myers, Richard, 196–97

Nahrein University, 20
Nairobi, 52
Najaf, 23, 48, 101, 110, 112–13, 136–37, 143, 151
Najjar, Mohammed, 152
Namani, Ali Hammad al, 92
napalm, 14, 18
Nassiriya, 48, 67
National Assembly of Kurdistan, 140
National Geographic, 77
National Guard, 24, 27, 80, 167
NATO, 51, 167
Negroponte, John, 33, 67, 150, 164, 165
New York Army National Guard, 167
New York Times, 34, 35, 90, 136, 149
NGOs, 19, 50, 115, 124
Nidal, Um, 121
Norway, 96, 97

Obeidi, Dhafer al, 34
oil, 24–25, 40, 72–73, 77, 142, 144, 146, 152, 174
Omar, Mullah, 106
Operation al Fajr, 31
Organization for the Freedom of Women in Iraq, 122, 124–25, 128–29
Ossola, 43
Othman, Mahmud, 147
Oxford Research Group, 71

pacifism, 11, 12, 51, 68, 85, 161, 171, 176
Pakistan, 38

Palau, Josep, 52
Palazzo Chigi, 155, 163, 171, 181–82
Palestine, 43, 70, 153, 187
Pari, Simona, 20, 59, 87
Parlato, Valentino, 170, 173
parliament, Iraqi, 129, 147
Party of the Democratic Left (DS), 170
Parwana, 98
pasdaran, 113
Patriotic Union of Kurdistan, 96, 140, 153
Pentagon, 7, 192, 195, 196, 197
Persians, 138
peshmerga, 97, 144, 146, 147
phosphorus, 14, 18
Piedmontese Valley, 43
Poland, 147
Pollari, Nicolo, 155, 156, 181, 182
Polo, Gabriele, 61, 155, 161, 170, 172, 178, 181, 182
Pope, 114, 161, 172
prisoner of war, 69

Qadisiyah, 138
Al Qaeda, 25, 96, 114, 136, 141
al Qaid elementary, 32
Qasem, Abdul , 112
Qatar, 24
Qom, 113, 152
Quaker, 11

Ra'ad, 87
Rabiah, 123
Ragaglini, Cesare, 163
RAI Channel 3 news, 169
Ramadan, 58, 109
Ramadhan, Taha Yassin, 92, 93
Ramadi, 66, 139
Rana, 128, 129
rape, 62, 124, 124, 126–28
Rashid, Harun al, 137
Rashid, Latif, 72, 74
Rawa, 98
Red Crescent, 22

Red Cross, Italian, 178
Red Sea, 54
religious police, 111
resistance, "Saddamist", 33
resistance, Giuliana's, 86, 87
resistance, Iraqi, 5, 18–19, 29, 31–32, 35, 65–66, 76, 83, 85, 86, 88–95, 114, 136–37, 139, 146, 148, 151, 187, 191
Ritter, Scott, 89–90
Roma, 56
Roman Catholic, 11
Rome, 15, 43–44, 57–59, 87, 107, 114, 159–61, 167, 173, 177, 192, 196–97, 199, 209, 211
Rome Auditorium, 177
al Rumaitha, 76
Rumsfeld, Donald, 196
Russia, 79, 108

Saad bin Abi Waqas Mosque, 34
Saddam City, 110, 112
Saddamist, 33
Sadeq, Mohammed, 112
Sadr City, 27, 34, 110, 112, 136, 137
al Sadr, Muqtada, 112–13, 130, 135, 137, 144, 149, 152
Salafists, 102, 108
Salaidin, 52
Saleh, Jassim Mohammed, 33
Samarra, 90, 139
Sarajevo, 52
Saudi, 34, 84, 114
Saudi Arabia, 84
Scelli, Maurizio, 178
Schiavo, Terri, 191
Scolari, Pier, 43, 53–55, 61, 86, 104, 119, 155, 159, 161, 169–70, 211
Sembler, Mel, 210
Serbo-Croatian, 158
Shakla, 127
Shalaklava, 52
Shari'a, 15, 33, 112–13, 129–30, 143, 145
Shatt al Arab, 76
Sheik Abdullah al Janabi, 34

Sheikh Hussein, 20–21, 23–27, 29, 34, 105
Shiite, 15, 23, 34–35, 71, 76, 95, 98, 101–102, 105, 110–14, 125, 129–30, 133–34, 136–39, 142–53
Shlash, Mihsin, 73
shura, 33
al Shurta, 74
SISMI—Italian Security and Military Service, 155, 163, 170–171, 176, 178–82
al Sistani, Ali, 95, 110, 112–13, 129, 133, 136, 139, 143, 151
Sites, Kevin, 18, 31
The Slavery of the Veil, 108
Small Arms Survey, 71
smart bombs, 10, 69
Sofia, 53
Soldiers of Islam, 96
soldiers, British, 149, 150
soldiers, Iranian, 152
soldiers, Iraqi, 35, 147
soldiers, U.S., 8, 13, 15, 31–32, 34, 51, 65, 67, 70, 77, 89, 126–27, 156–57, 160, 162–67, 181, 187–88, 191–95, 198–200
Somalia, 10, 21, 43, 52, 170, 187, 206
Sowera, 128
Spaniards, 51
Star Wars, 30
suicide bombing, 92, 93, 97, 108, 137
Sulaimaniya, 124, 125, 135
Sumerians, 76, 187
al Sunna, Ansar, 97–98
Sunni, 15, 20, 23, 31, 34, 69, 93, 94, 95, 96, 97, 98, 102, 105, 110, 111, 113, 114, 125, 133–39, 14–146, 148, 150–51, 153
Sunni Triangle, 96, 98, 146, 148
Supreme Council for the Islamic Revolution (SCIRI), 110, 113, 129, 143, 150–52
Sydney, 10
Syria, 73, 77, 115

Tajik mujahideen, 117
Talabani, Jalal, 96, 97, 141, 153

Taliban, 34, 52, 95–96, 98, 104, 106, 117–18, 121
Tarmia Plant, 75
al Tawheed, 136
Tawhid, 97
Tehran, 113, 147, 151–53
Texas, 73
Third Infantry Brigade, 127
Third Infantry Division, 209
Tikrit, 97
Times, the, 80
Torretta, Simona, 19, 59, 87
Totti, Francesco, 56, 173
Turkey, 21, 73, 77
Turkmen, 141, 142
Tuwaitha, 78
Tuwaitha Center for Nuclear Research, 78–79

U.S. Central Command, 70
Ulema, 93, 95, 114, 133, 144, 153
Ulema, Council of the, 93, 95, 114, 133
Um al Marik, 92
Um al Marik Mosque, 109
UN, 76
unilaterals, 7
United Iraqi Alliance, 139
United Nations Environmental Program Task Force, 78
United Nations Integrated Regional Information Network, 75
UNSCOM, 89

Vangjel Commission, 167
Vangjel, Peter, 163
veil, 24, 108, 111, 114, 119, 123, 130–31
al velayat e faqih, 113
Veltroni, Walter, 173, 211
Vietnam, 34, 66, 80, 83
Vincent, Steven, 149

Wahhabist, 24, 34, 96–97, 102, 105, 107, 114, 134, 143
Waqf, 150

Warda, Pascale, 115
Wardhia, 79
World Food Program, 118
World Resources Institute, 77

Yarmuk, 74
Yarmuk Hospital, 150
Yawar, Ghazi al, 139
Younes, Talib Abu, 75
Yugoslavia, 51, 135

Zakya, Khalifa, 121
Zarqawi, Abu Mussab al, 25, 34, 88, 97–98, 102, 136, 146

ABOUT HAYMARKET BOOKS

Haymarket Books is a nonprofit, progressive book distributor and publisher, a project of the Center for Economic Research and Social Change. We believe that activists need to take ideas, history, and politics into the many struggles for social justice today. Learning the lessons of past victories, as well as defeats, can arm a new generation of fighters for a better world. As Karl Marx said, "The philosophers have merely interpreted the world; the point however is to change it."

We take inspiration and courage from our namesakes, the Haymarket Martyrs, who gave their lives fighting for a better world. Their 1886 struggle for the eight-hour day, which gave us May Day, the international workers' holiday, reminds workers around the world that ordinary people can organize and struggle for their own liberation. These struggles continue today across the globe—struggles against oppression, exploitation, hunger, and poverty.

For more information, visit www.haymarketbooks.org

Distributed to the trade by Consortium Book Sales and Distribution, www.cbsd.org

ALSO FROM HAYMARKET BOOKS

A Little Piece of Ground
Elizabeth Laird • The experience of the Israeli occupation of Palestine through the eyes of a twelve-year-old boy. ISBN 1931859388.

A People's History of Iraq: The Iraqi Communist Party, Workers' Movements, and the Left 1924–2004
Ilario Salucci • Iraqis have a long tradition of fighting against foreign and domestic tyranny. Here is their story. ISBN 1931859140.

No One Is Illegal: Fighting Racism and State Violence on the Border
Justin Akers Chacón and Mike Davis • *No One Is Illegal* debunks the leading ideas behind the often violent right-wing backlash against immigrants.

Subterranean Fire: A History of Working-Class Radicalism in the U.S.
Sharon Smith • *Subterranean Fire* brings working-class history to light and reveals its lessons for today. ISBN 193185923X.